BECOMING A
MANAGER

Thoughts & Tools for
Your Transition

Learning from Experienced Managers

PATRICK CUNNEEN

·OAK·TREE·PRESS·

Published by OAK TREE PRESS, 19 Rutland Street, Cork, Ireland

www.oaktreepress.com

© 2011 Patrick Cunneen

A catalogue record of this book is available from the British Library.

ISBN 978 1 904887 73 7 (ePub)
ISBN 978 1 904887 74 4 (Kindle)
ISBN 978 1 904887 75 1 (paperback)
ISBN 978 1 904887 85 0 (hardback)

Cover design: Kieran O'Connor Design
Cover illustration: Vance Vasu / Getty Images
Internal illustrations: Ken Lee

CONTENTS

DEDICATION

To Jacinta

ACKNOWLEDGEMENTS

I have enjoyed unstinting and patient support from my colleagues and family throughout the development and writing of this book.

In particular, the book would not have been possible without the ready willingness of busy managers to give me their time to be interviewed. My sincere thanks to all of them, for sharing their experiences and insights honestly and openly, warts and all.

I also wish to thank my colleagues for their support and endless patience. Thanks to Thérèse Brady, Eamon Ryan and Tom Finucane and thanks to my family, Jacinta, Deirdre, Niamh and Eoghan.

I am particularly grateful to Brian O'Kane, managing director of Oak Tree Press, for his faith in the book and for his excellent contribution as editor.

INTRODUCTION

For over three decades, across three continents, I have enjoyed a most interesting and satisfying career helping to select, support and develop managers. This included recruiting young college graduates from campus and supporting many of them to make their own transitions into management.

Through some excellent networks developed with many of these and managers in other organisations, I am fortunate to have access to a wide selection of successful practicing managers; practical managers who are capable of reflection on their careers and the careers of those around them; managers who have been happy to share their early management experiences and insights with me, warts and all! This experience and insight hopefully will make the book interesting to a broad international audience.

Having said that, the content of the book largely reflects Western management principles and practices. There are many countries in the world where quite different values and behaviours are clearly evident and managers with international responsibilities need to build the cross-cultural sensitivity and skills required for today's global business environment.

Young professionals, who spent all their college education learning about fluid dynamics, semiconductors, discounted cash flows or the law of torts, and then spent their early career years applying that learning as individual contributors, have had little opportunity to study and practise being a manager; becoming a boss. They have had little opportunity to understand and reflect upon the necessary transition to a new and very different role as a manager.

The Focus of this Book

In most societies in the Western world, ambitious young professionals work hard to be promoted and promotion is seen as a validation of career success. For many employees, their first significant promotion involves taking on responsibility for the supervision and management of other people.

However, what is less understood is that the new role is fundamentally different from the old one. Whether you work in industry, professional services, the public service, or not-for-profit organisations, this *transition* into a management role can be greatly underestimated. There is much more involved than a new title, office or salary increase. It involves a deeper understanding of what is required to be successful in your new role, together with an increased level of self-awareness and new skills.

There are lots of books and training seminars on the tools and techniques of effective supervision and management for newly promoted managers. However, before you can learn and apply these techniques, it is essential to understand that your job has changed in a most fundamental way.

Part One of this book explores the essential *transition* that takes place from being an individual contributor and team player to becoming a manager; from being focused on your own work to being focused on the work of others.

Use this book to carefully consider the nature and scope of your new responsibilities. You are not a 'plug and play' capability that the organisation has put in place. You have a great opportunity to learn and grow in your new role and provide important leadership in the performance improvement of your new team. Consider the advice and experience of a wide range of highly successful and insightful managers recalled and explored through the following chapters.

Once you have reflected on the changed nature, scope and scale of your new role, **Part Two** goes on to highlight and explain important skills and competencies in managing people. Use this part of the book not just as an initial primer for managing people but as a useful reference guide or 'tool kit' to remind and support you on essential skills that you will require on a regular basis into the future.

The general body of the book reflects the 'harvesting' of experience and insights from the managers I interviewed, together with the many conversations I have had with managers across decades and continents. Where relevant, I have included quotations from these managers – which I believe add greatly to the learning to be drawn from this book. However, in order to preserve anonymity, a pre-condition of the interview process at the outset, the name of the manager attached to each quotation is fictitious, though their broad industry sector and country are correct.

Becoming an excellent manager is not a destination. It is a never-ending journey; a journey of opportunity for continuous learning and personal growth. When you 'boil down' the book, you will not find much that is fundamentally new that will test your understanding of leadership and management. Hopefully, in its place, you will find an opportunity to reflect on seasoned sound practical advice and good common sense.

Who is this Book for?

Becoming a Manager is primarily oriented towards professionals who are interested in developing their careers in management and those who have recently been promoted into such roles. The key objective is to help and support them through their transitions into management. The book should also be helpful to would-be entrepreneurs, considering starting their own business.

The book is also targeted at HR and Employee Development departments to assist them in creating effective transitional training programmes and materials for new and emerging managers, as they seek to attract, develop and retain management talent.

PART 1

MAKING THE TRANSITION

**A different role: The conductor no longer plays
an instrument in the orchestra**

CHAPTER 1

DIFFERENT JOB, DIFFERENT SKILLS

Congratulations on your promotion! This is a time of celebration, excitement *and* transition. An essential part of that transition needs to be the realisation that your job has changed fundamentally. You may still be in the same organisation, even in the same department; but that is where the similarities stop. Your old and your new job are as different as chalk and cheese.

Your promotion to manager is not unlike a talented musician trading his or her instrument for a conductor's baton. You no longer play that instrument in the orchestra. The conductor coordinates and perhaps even inspires the work of others to collaborate in producing a perfectly synchronised musical production. So, you too now need to lead and manage the work of others.

Of course, not every organisation has a clear definition of the role and responsibilities of a manager. For many, the role is understood simply as the list of tasks to be completed: manage and control budgets, resolve technical difficulties that arise, ship X number of widgets per month, supervise consultants, issue client reports, etc. Not surprisingly, new managers often find themselves grappling with the question: "What is my job anyway?"

So, what is the role of a manager? While you will always have to balance the technical demands and budgetary requirements of your department, your new and fundamentally different role as a manager is to get results through *other* people. For example,

Proctor & Gamble, a successful international consumables firm for over 100 years, leaves no room for ambiguity regarding the role of their managers. P&G expects its managers to create and lead a positive environment for performance improvement; to foster creativity and have a healthy disregard for conventional thinking; and to embrace change and be rigorous in the execution of planned goals.

Letting Go

Many of the managers I have interviewed for this book mentioned that letting go of the old job was one of the biggest challenges they had. Consciously or otherwise, there can be quite a degree of tree-hugging to the old job and its obvious comfort zone. After all, it was their performance in their old job that generated the recognition that lead to their promotion. However, to swing on a circus trapeze, you must let go of one bar before you can reach out and catch the new bar swinging towards you. You need to make a clean and deliberate mental break from your old job and grasp the challenge and opportunity of the new one. You need to leave the old job and your comfort zone behind as you stretch out towards your new role and responsibilities.

> *There are very real dangers of continuing to do what you have been good at and recognised for. People are very slow to move out of their comfort zone. Things have moved on (your job has changed) and you have to change too.*
> Mark, Key Account Manager, Financial Services, US

There is perhaps an understandable temptation to hold onto aspects of your old job. Undoubtedly, there can be a sense of gratification when you respond satisfactorily to an urgent matter as you did in the past. In the very short term, you may enjoy the satisfaction of the moment, but you quickly will find out that you have taken on too much yourself and neither your old nor new role will be done to anyone's satisfaction.

> *Because I was trying so hard to impress, I micro-managed everything during that first year in the mistaken belief that I knew best how to do it. I ended up driving myself into the ground and everyone else nuts. Another consequence of my approach was that two of the best people in the department transferred out during that time.*
> Jessica, Department Manager, Financial Services, UK

A Transition

Your transition into management is likely to be one of the most challenging times in your professional life. The early months are crucial as they can have a disproportionate effect on your success in your new role. First impressions do count. Your capacity to manage the transition successfully will make a lasting impression. Unfortunately, the opposite result leaves an even longer lasting impression! Poor transitions result in poor outcomes for the organisation, for your new employees and most importantly, for you!

> *When I made the transition to becoming a manager, the first thing I did was to recognise that I now had a different job. I'd moved from position A to position B so I thought very carefully about what I needed to know about position B to allow me to be successful in my new role. While you may get some help from the organisation, the only person who can reflect on the changed situation and the requirements is yourself.*
> Kevin, Senior Manager, Government Agency, Ireland

Change is not the same as transition. Change is an *event*: a promotion, a new boss, the arrival of a first child. Transition, on the other hand, is a *process*. It is a process over time, which is necessary to get used to the new reality; a coming to terms with the change that has taken place. This is a critical time when either you begin to gain some traction with your colleagues or you just spin your wheels. You can generate much of that essential traction by achieving early wins through delegating your old work to others, releasing you to focus on and lead towards the achievement of your 'vital few' important goals.

> *I found the transition very challenging. I was younger with less life experience and found myself managing older, more experienced people. I survived through a tough transition because I sought out the support and sound advice I received from a couple of senior colleagues during those early months.*
> Greg, VP Operations, US

The Dangers of a Two-Step Transition

For some people, the transition into management can be a two-step process. The initial step is characterised by continuing to do the technical aspects of your work but now taking a few more junior personnel 'under your wing' and giving them general guidance, direction and support. The second step is very different and more pronounced, in that you take on direct and more formal responsibility for the performance of the individual. You also become a major influence in their career development. Step 1 might be likened to being an older sibling, while step 2 is more like being a parent. Do not assume that, as step 1 is such a relatively easy evolution, step 2 will be the same; it is a much more pronounced and challenging step-up.

One manager warned:

> *Because the transition into the first phase of supervision was so easy and felt so natural, I simply wasn't prepared for the second transition into more formal management and it took me a very long time to figure out that there was a big difference.*
> Marcus, VP Operations, US

Another manager agreed:

> *It's very easy to slide into the phase 1 of managing others. It allows you to stay in your old comfort zone. One manager I knew evolved into a role managing a software architecture team. However, as the job grew and his management role became more demanding, he slipped back more and more into his technical comfort zone and eventually was replaced in the manager role.*
> Jonathan, Software Development Manager, High-Tech, UK

You need to be alert to the much bigger transition and challenges involved in this second step.

The Hard Stuff is Easy, It's the Soft Stuff that's Hard

One of the most fundamental shifts in your new role is your direct involvement with your employees and other groups. Ray Stata, co-founder and chairman of Analog Devices Inc., regularly warned his managers of the seeming paradox that 'the hard stuff is easy, it's the soft stuff that's hard'. Technical challenges are easier to define and resolve. Interpersonal challenges are much more demanding because people are multi-dimensional and complex and no two are the same.

> " *I slowly came to realise the importance of organisational awareness — how to get things done in the organisation; not only how to manage downwards but upwards and sideways just as well! I had been gloriously unaware of the need to manage upwards; the absolute need for clarity on priorities; and some understanding about how to build influence and get things done.* "
> Greg, VP Operations, US

As a newly promoted manager, you have proved yourself to be highly capable and hard-working as an individual contributor. The key to your continued success now is to make the psychological adjustment in your new managerial role and begin to master the new skills required. In his widely acclaimed book *Emotional Intelligence*, Daniel Goleman[1] describes his research of managerial skills and competencies across 188 companies. In that study, he categorised skills into three dimensions: technical (for example, engineering, IT, accounting, etc.), cognitive (analytical thinking, logic, etc.) and interpersonal skills. Using quite objective criteria, he found that, beyond a certain career stage, differences in technical and cognitive skills became less of a differentiator of management success than interpersonal skills. In other words, you obviously require a good base-line level of technical and cognitive skills to do the job; however, it is the interpersonal skills that make the difference as you progress further into management.

A study of 385 managers at the Personal Care Division of Johnson & Johnson indicated that the highest performing

---

[1]   Goleman, D. (1996). *Emotional Intelligence*, London: Bloomsbury Publishing.

managers had significantly more 'emotional competence' or interpersonal skills than other managers.[2]

In today's ever flatter, downsized organisations, individuals are often thrown into management roles with little preparation and even less support. Flatter organisations also suggest that the promotional steps are steeper with even greater transitional challenges. One of the biggest difficulties facing these new managers is that, unfortunately, many organisations just throw you into the deep end of the pool and let you 'sink or swim' on your own. This attitude, on the part of more senior management, assumes that you will 'figure it out, just as we had to do'. If you encounter a similar situation of being thrown into the deep-end with little or no direct support then it is very important for you to recognise this from the 'get go' and look for a few 'friendly faces' and begin to build an informal network for advice and counsel.

> *It's very time-consuming to build that network of relationships, but it is essential that you do invest the time to do it.*
> **Gene, Regional Director, Pharma, South-East Asia**

Organisations need to understand the critical transition into management and to provide early training and support to new managers. Indeed the role of the organisation starts much earlier than the training phase. Organisations need to be thoughtful in their judgement as to who they select for promotion into management – that the potential candidate has demonstrated some evidence that they can be a good manager and manage the

---

[2]   Cavallo, K. & Brienza, D. (2007). *Emotional Competence and Leadership Excellence at Johnson & Johnson: The Emotional Intelligence and Leadership Study*, Consortium for Research on Emotional Intelligence, Sea Girt, NJ: Corporate Consulting Group.

transition effectively. Not surprisingly, the organisational defence when a new manager fails to swim, having been 'thrown in at the deep end', often is that it is the new manager's fault: "he / she didn't cut it". Rarely is there some self-reflection that asks "Did we promote the right person?" or "Did we support and guide the new manager sufficiently early on?" So little or no organisational learning takes place, allowing the situation to repeat itself easily in the future.

Conclusion

A transition into management begins with a clear understanding that your job has changed; that your role is different. Before your new team start to see you as a leader, you must see yourself first as a leader. The skills and other characteristics that served you well in the past, resulting in this promotion, now need to be supplemented with other skills and competencies. However, the starting point is an acknowledgement to yourself that your job and your responsibilities have changed; that things indeed have moved on.

Interpersonal skills such as influencing, negotiating, listening and communicating, giving feedback and coaching, managing conflict and discipline become the essential currency for your career development going forward from this first management promotion.

CHAPTER 2

ADVICE FOR EARLY ON

Most of **Chapter 1** was devoted to explaining that your job has changed fundamentally. It encouraged you to let go of your old role – to focus on people and not just tasks. Accepting that advice and coming to terms with the transition are the foundation for developing your new managerial career. Beyond that fundamental change, the following advice is offered to help you through the early months of your transition and to put a solid foundation during the early weeks and months in your new role.

Becoming a Manager is Not a Sprint

Becoming a manager is not a sprint; it is a marathon. You need time to think about your new role and possible approaches; to take time to begin to build relationships. Managers I have spoken with all warn against getting caught in an activity trap very early, sometimes getting into a hectic activity cycle and being unable to think clearly. It is both understandable and easy to take on too much during your transition; however, the results can be quite damaging to you and the organisation.

In my own transitions across roles and countries, I have always tried to carve out time early on to talk and listen to my new team members as well as peers / internal customers. Only when you have had a chance to understand the various stakeholders and their issues are you in a position to begin to develop relationships and plans for the future.

66   *You need to take time to listen and understand. There's*
      an understandable inclination to go immediately to
      "DO" mode. But you do that at your peril. Whether it's
      getting to know your new employees or your peer
      groups, you need to spend some time listening to
      understand.   99
Gene, Regional Director, Pharma, South-East Asia

On promotion, some managers immediately go about changing the things that they have long believed needed changing. The managers I interviewed would urge you not to do that.

66   *No, you need to be a little patient and to think long and*
      carefully about what needs to change. You need to show
      respect for the past and begin to build challenges for the
      future together. People won't necessarily welcome
      change and you need to bring them with you. But the
      very first step is to listen to people.   99
Marcus, VP Operations, US

There is a danger of course of taking this advice as an excuse to do nothing in the short-term, which leads us to another piece of important advice.

Do Not Put Off the Obvious

Experienced managers warn against putting off actions that need to be addressed early in your new job. One manager reflected that he had made a serious mistake in not addressing an employee relations problem early. So, by the time he finally faced up to dealing with the problem, it had become a much more serious disciplinary issue, resulting in much more time and effort to resolve the matter.

> *There was an obvious problem with one employee. He had bid for the same promotion opportunity and was clearly unhappy when I was given the job. He started playing games and testing me on minor disciplinary issues. For a while I ignored the situation, hoping that time would fix the problem but it only got worse. Of course all the other employees were watching this tennis ping-pong between the two of us, wondering if I was ever going to deal with the issue. In the end, I had no choice but to confront the situation but now the situation was much more serious than had I addressed the problem earlier on. My mistake was waiting six months trying to preserve the status quo and trying to keep everyone happy. The reality was that nobody was happy with the situation.*
> Mark, Key Account Manager, Financial Services, US

In situations where there is an obvious problem, it is important to assess the situation as carefully as you can. Seek advice from a few people you trust for their experience and commonsense. Where available, seek advice from your HR advisor and then take the necessary action.

> *I've seen new managers make the mistake of not looking for help when a new and difficult situation arises. There's bound to be someone who's seen it all before and can give you advice.*
> Gene, Regional Director, Pharma, South-East Asia

Sometimes a 'full and frank' exchange of views is all that is necessary to clear the air and clarify expectations. Putting off the obvious only breeds uncertainty and potential unpleasantness for all.

Delegate and Empower

Trying to do everything yourself is a fool's game. Effective delegation gives you that precious commodity of time – time to focus on the more important issues.

Some new managers, in 'DO' mode, convince themselves that they can get the task done more quickly than having to show somebody else how to do it. While that might be true on the first occasion, what about the second, third and subsequent times the task arises? Making an initial investment in the time to train an employee in a task is likely to yield huge dividends in saving time in the future as this task can now be delegated effectively to your employee. The additional benefit is that the employee is likely to feel that they are learning new skills and more likely to want to stick around.

> 66 *The team were working on a solution to a problem. I understood the problem and felt that I had a much better solution than the one evolving from the team. It was really difficult for me not to wade into the middle of the team with my fireman's helmet and axe and tell them how to fix it. But I bit my tongue and waited and they came up with a novel approach and showed great commitment in implementing their solution.* 99
> **Bryan, Director, Management Consulting, Ireland**

Managers who do not delegate effectively not only end up in never-ending 'activity traps' but typically have much higher levels of staff turnover as people leave because they feel they are not getting job satisfaction from doing only the more mundane and trivial tasks. They leave because they do not feel they are learning or developing their careers.

It has been said that a perfectionist is one who takes great pains … and often gives them to other people! Success in management is not about your individual contribution; it is about getting the best out of the collective efforts and intellectual horsepower of the team. A 90% solution developed by the team, implemented with their active commitment (because it is *their* solution) is likely to have a more successful outcome than your 100% solution which the team is instructed to implement.

There are of course employees who will only be too pleased to have their manager do all the work and make all the decisions. One manager I interviewed spoke of a frustrating experience he had taking over a new department:

> " *Early on, several of my employees regularly brought their problems to me, asking me what I thought. I described the practice at the time as 'bringing dead birds to my door'. To address the problem, I raised the issue at a staff meeting and explained that I expected these employees to deal with these issues themselves; they were well capable of dealing with the vast majority of problems and certainly well paid to do so! I even had a special sign made up, reading 'No Dead Birds', which I put on my desk.* "
> Jeff, Division VP, High-tech, US

Some employees may take the negative view that you are delegating down and letting them do the 'dirty work'. However, there is an organisational reality that requires you to delegate. Time is a scarce resource and delegation of tasks gives you more time to focus on the important issues that need to be addressed. Not to delegate will have you rushing about in never-ending, time-consuming activity traps. Having said that, good managers always are prepared to roll up their sleeves and get stuck-in on a task with their employees in a crisis situation, thereby demonstrating their willingness to get their hands dirty and help out. However, this should be very much the exception and not the rule. Effective delegation is a demonstration of trust and confidence in your employees and provides them with opportunities for building new skills.

> " *One of the hardest things I had to do when I became a manager was to leave it to others to perform the task and fix the problem. The instant gratification of fixing the problem that I used to enjoy so much goes away. You're now the cheer-leader of others.* "
> Edward, Director, Manufacturing Operations, Ireland

If you find yourself grumbling about a growing work-load, ask yourself the question: "Am I delegating enough?" Delegating effectively means you get to focus less on performing tasks and more on planning and leading. It is not as much about personal achievement any more as it is about enabling others to achieve. You have given up playing a musical instrument; you are now conducting the orchestra.

Employees are Different – Treat Them Differently

Intuitively, it seems only right, from a fairness and equity standpoint, that you would want to treat each of your employees exactly the same.

However, no two of your employees are exactly the same; no two situations are exactly alike. As a consequence, there is no single best style of management: it all depends. Effective managers adapt their own style of management to suit the skill and motivational level of their employees.

Hersey & Blanchard[3] suggest that a manager needs to be good at analysing situations and at adapting their approach given that analysis. The amount of active supervision and encouragement

---

[3]   Hersey, P. and Blanchard, K. (1972). *Management of Organisational Behaviour: Utilizing Human Resources*, New Jersey: Prentice Hall.

depends to a great extent on the skill capability of the employee and their level of personal motivation. A new employee probably will be highly motivated; however, their skill level may be on the low side. In this case, you need to supervise their operation very carefully. On the other hand, you can delegate much to an employee who is highly skilled, confident and motivated.

> " *You can be a safe manager if you treat everyone the same but you probably won't be a very good one. Too little supervision will create an environment where an inexperienced employee will make too many mistakes, be stressed and probably quit prematurely; too much supervision and an experienced employee will feel they are being micro-managed. It all depends.* "
> Bryan, Director, Management Consulting, Ireland

Spend time assessing the skills, capabilities and motivational levels of your employees. Then, and only then, are you in a position to adapt your management style and approach to suit the situation.

However, be warned that when you apply these different management styles for different people, it is very important that you explain to them why you are using different approaches. If you have a highly skilled and motivated employee and you delegate tasks to them and then disappear, they may begin to wonder "What did I do wrong? I never see my boss". Your approach to these different situations is something you should explain to your employees – different strokes for different folks.

Listen Carefully

By definition, new managers have neither all the knowledge nor the experience to make all the decisions that they are confronted with every day on their own. Given that, surely it makes sense to draw on the collective experience and wisdom of others. However, some new managers worry that asking other people for their ideas and opinions is a sign of weakness; an undermining of their own authority.

Careful listening and enquiry are essential skills of managers at all levels. A capacity to listen and question carefully does not undermine authority. Rather, it is an important process of information gathering before moving to decisions.

In seeking opinions of others, it is important to avoid only listening to the voices that are working to ingratiate themselves with you as their new boss. There is nothing more dangerous for a manager than to be surrounded by 'Yes-people'. Managers need to seek out the contrarian view in order to get as much balance in input as possible. To do that effectively means being open to ideas, encouraging different views and making it safe for people to offer views that are different to your own. To welcome ideas that are different to your own is not easy and we can privately dismiss them too readily.

There may be an inclination to seek out a person in your group as a confidant, who was a friend when you were peers in the past. You need to be very careful to avoid this or you risk a charge of creating an 'old pals' inner sanctum. Members of your team need equal access to you and to be seen to get that access.

> *Chemistry in relationships is a reality. Some people come into your office and you can chat for ages. Others come in and you immediately think "Aagh, how long will this take?" However, this person's input might be the most important input that day.*
> **Edward, Director, Manufacturing Operations, Ireland**

As you transition into management, it is essential that you take the time to enquire and listen carefully. What you hear is likely to be an interesting mix of facts, opinions and agendas. Your job is to listen carefully, separate the 'wheat from the chaff' and then and only then move to your decisions.

Careful listening and enquiry are essential skills of successful managers at all levels. Developing sound listening skills will be explored further in **Chapter 8**.

It is OK to Say "I do not Know"

Some new managers feel that if they appear not to have all the answers immediately, they will lose credibility and authority.

Clearly, it is hardly a good start for any new manager to say "I do not know" on a very regular basis. But you have been promoted based on your performance to-date and future potential – use that knowledge, experience and your growing judgement to answer the many questions and issues that arise every day.

> *We make a mistake when we try to look clever in front of our employees and pretend that we know everything. Inevitably, something's going to arise, especially in our managerial careers, when we won't know the answer and we try to wing it. You wing it at your peril. If you don't know the answer, say so.*
> Mark, Key Account Manager, Financial Services, US

Inevitably, there will be situations where important questions or situations arise that need answers: answers that you do not have. In those very real situations, some managers struggle with saying that they do not know. All the managers I interviewed agreed that it is OK to say "I don't know" in such situations but recommended that you commit to letting people know at the earliest possible time and then deliver on that commitment.

> *Our general manager announced that we would be off-shoring certain processes in 12 months' time and that there would probably be lay-offs / redundancies as a result but that he could not estimate the precise number at this time. As soon as we got back to our department, naturally I was inundated with concerns and queries as to what this meant for our group. I explained that I did not know the impact of that decision at that stage because our processing demands were very dynamic and that it might even be possible that sufficient new opportunities would arise elsewhere in the organisation in the meantime. I told the employees that I did not have the answer at that stage but I committed to meeting with them every quarter and updating them on developments and any emerging growth opportunities.*
> **Jessica, Department Manager, Financial Services, UK**

Where the answer is less clear and likely to remain so for some time, then commit to a process of regular updates.

Maintaining Close Friendships with Former Peers

This can be a really difficult transitional challenge. All the managers I interviewed agreed that it is not a good idea to try to carry on your friendships as if nothing has happened. Something has happened; you are now their boss!

> *In making the transition, you need to have some professional distance between yourself and your employees. If you maintain a familiarity and 'buddy-like' relationship, you may run the risk of being seen to be close to some employees to the detriment of your relationship with others. It also will be more difficult to deal with performance issues when these situations arise, as they inevitably do.*
> **Kevin, Senior Manager, Government Agency, Ireland**

> *This was one of the most difficult challenges I had to navigate through. I wanted to create a new relationship: one that was still friendly and collegiate but not 'buddy buddy' as it probably was in the past. Some of the people understood what I was trying to do and were OK with it; a few resented the situation. I don't know if that was a bit of professional jealousy or what. I continued to join the group for lunch but started to avoid events outside of work such as bowling or golf, especially if it was with a small subset of the total group and, doubly so, if there was drink involved. I was acutely aware that what might look like friendship to me might look like playing favourites to others.*
>
> John, Product Development Manager, Technology, US

This situation is often more difficult and awkward for your team members than it is for you. A real and mature friend will understand the dilemma that you both face and make an effort to work with you to establish a new relationship without a word ever having been spoken. Some people will accept that you are now their manager and get on with it. Others will struggle with your efforts to transition to a new and different relationship. These may need an honest and sincere exchange of views before coming around to the new reality. Sadly, there may be somebody who will only resolve his or her issue with you by moving department or even organisation. However, that is ultimately their problem to resolve not yours.

> *There will be difficult decisions ahead and you need to create some distance, not by being stand-offish but by building respect and credibility. You've got to stand up and be credible.*
>
> Greg, VP Operations, US

Of course, you can err at the other extreme too, where you are more demanding on your old friends in order to demonstrate to everybody how independent and unbiased you are.

> *One manager I observed was really tough with his former friends, I think just to show how independent and fair he was to everyone else. One by one those friends quit but interestingly, others did too because they felt that you couldn't rely on any loyalty from the guy. After all, just look at what he did to his friends.*
> John, Product Development Manager, Technology, US

> *I've seen a few managers in my time blowing their newly acquired sense of power totally out of proportion changing from being a tried and trusted colleague and friend to being the greatest monster ever.*
> Gene, Regional Director, Pharma, South-East Asia

All the managers I interviewed agreed that it is possible to evolve new relationships: relationships that are still friendly and collegiate. It is important to clarify to your friends what they can expect from you in the way you interact with every member of your department or team. You need to hold them individually and collectively accountable for meeting their goals; living to common practices and procedures for everyone.

Be Sure to Manage Up as Well as Down

Managing upwards is a critical skill at almost any time but it is essential during the early months following your promotion. The reality is that your boss probably does not have a lot of time to sit around and interact with you. He or she is likely to be juggling many different customers, processes or projects.

> *Many new managers don't seem to realise that*
> *managing their boss is very much their responsibility.*
> *They often don't understand the breadth of their boss's*
> *responsibilities and interests. Your team depends on you*
> *to manage your relationship with your boss effectively.*
> *Your team will be much more successful if you are*
> *successful in managing your boss.*
> Greg, VP Operations, US

On the face of it, 'managing your boss' can sound somewhat political and manipulative. That is not what is intended here. Managing your boss is really about effective upward communications:

- Appreciate the time demands on your boss: find time-efficient ways to keep him or her informed of progress.

- Provide regular updates to those plans.

- Keep your boss informed of important issues that arise and what you plan to do about them.

- Present your proposals clearly and concisely, with facts and not just opinions to back up your proposals.

- If you sense your boss is negative towards your proposal, do not drive for closure. Suggest that he / she have a think about it and come back to the proposal another day – 'those who fight and run away, live to fight another day'.

- Most importantly, quickly come to understand how your manager absorbs information. If your manager is 'big picture', then do not drown him or her in lots of details and minutiae. Equally, do not speak in generalities if your boss wants to see the detail. Sense how the conversation is going. If you begin to see glazed eyes, change gear and quickly get to the point.

> " *One of the biggest mistakes I made early on in my new managerial job was that I didn't calibrate certain priorities with my new boss. It's not to say that we didn't sit down and discuss certain goals. We did. However, I failed to bring clarity to my approach to some priorities over others; I didn't help him to understand the implications of prioritising one activity over another.* "
>
> Mark, Key Account Manager, Financial Services, US

> " *I found a good time to chat with and update my boss was mid-afternoon on a Friday when usually things were calming down a bit and he was more likely to be in a more reflective state of mind.* "
>
> Jessica, Dept. Manager, Financial Services, UK

Given the ever-increasing complexity in organisations, many larger international companies have introduced matrix or dual reporting structures. In such a structure, you are likely to report to different bosses for different roles or geographies. This certainly makes the concept of managing your boss much more difficult, given their possible conflicting objectives and priorities.

> " *I think I'm a collaborative person but I had two matrixed managers with very different priorities. It was a challenge to keep them both on-side with what I was doing and what my priorities were. I think you need enlightened self-interest and to keep the lines of communication active and open all the time.* "
>
> Jonathan, Software Development Manager, High-Tech, UK

It has been said that matrix management is less about structure and more about a frame of mind. Your challenge is to work to achieve a common frame of mind between yourself and these matrixed managers. It requires a high level of collaboration, cooperation and continuous communications between each of you.

Conclusion

In reading this early advice, you could be forgiven for thinking that the transition into management is too challenging. There is no doubt that it is challenging but it is also exciting. This transition is very much your launch pad to develop your managerial career. In promoting you, your organisation has given you a huge vote of confidence. They obviously believe in you – believe in yourself.

CHAPTER 3

IMPORTANT VALUES AND BEHAVIOURS FOR TRANSITION

There is a deeply personal challenge in taking on the responsibility to lead others. This challenge is less about skills, which can be learned and much more to do with you and your personal values and behaviours. Too often tacit or assumed, these values and behaviour are about who you are and what you stand for. They include being honest and straight with people; fairness and equity; respect for people's dignity at work; being accountable; showing appreciation; and most importantly, leading by example.

Being Authentic

Love it or hate it, the BBC series *The Office* was one of Britain's favourite comedies for several years. In the series, Ricky Gervais brutally lampoons leadership behaviour. In one episode, he announces that the Slough office is going to be merged and that there will be job losses. Totally oblivious to the palpable concern and fear that he has just introduced into the group, Gervais blissfully goes on to announce that he has just been promoted and waits for them to congratulate him.

As Gervais moved on to talk about something that scarcely interested them (his promotion), his staff were still processing and reacting to the news of impending job redundancies. As a manager, you need to be able to put yourself in the shoes of your employees and try to understand their concerns and their fears. A little bit of empathy and understanding goes a long way.

Being authentic means ... being honest and straight with people. Most employees respond well to straight-talking managers. They may not always like what they hear from you but they will respect the fact that you are being straight with them. A recurring theme from many different employment surveys is that employees value leading by example and honesty as two of the most important traits in a leader. More than anything else, employees want their manager to be straight and honest with them.

Being authentic means ... that you value your employees' opinions and give those opinions due consideration.

> *One of the nicest compliments you can pay someone is to ask "What do you think?" However, be careful! You can't go to the well too often and not drink the water. If you ask for suggestions or opinions, you must be prepared to accept them, at least some of the time.*
> Jean, Supply Chain Manager, Pharma, UK

Being authentic means ... being prepared to say "No" when it is necessary. When you have to say "No", do not beat about the bush or be tentative in any way. You can be assertive in saying "No" without being aggressive. Explain your reason(s) clearly. Remind your employees that you will not always agree on everything. Be careful as well to not discourage them from bringing you other proposals and suggestions in the future.

Being authentic also means saying "No" when you know you cannot deliver. Too often people nod their assent to something that they have no ability to deliver on. Too much time and money is wasted and too many expectations are frustrated when people are not honest and do not say "No" when they need to.

Saying "No" may be unpopular, especially with your boss, but paradoxically, it can help you build trust when you can demonstrate sound logic and reason for your dissenting voice. Group-think is a dangerous potion for any management team.

Being authentic means ... being fair and equitable to your employees. However, being fair and treating everyone the same is not the same thing. No two of your employees are exactly the same; no two situations are exactly alike. To treat two employees delivering two very different levels of performance with the same rewards and recognition is hardly fair. It is very important not only to be fair but to be seen to be fair. When you make decisions that can affect people, or their role and responsibilities, make sure to explain your rationale. They may not agree with you but will appreciate you explaining your position and more likely be accepting of it.

Being authentic means ... being willing to confront difficult issues. Side-stepping, putting off or ignoring an important issue in the hope that it goes away is likely to come back to haunt you later. In the long-run, nobody benefits if you sweep important issues under the carpet.

Being authentic means ... that you respect people's personal dignity. If you have to confront a difficult situation or have to take serious action, you can do so and still preserve people's dignity. It is possible to be assertive and yet be respectful at the same time. Treat others as you would like to be treated yourself under similar circumstances.

Being authentic means ... being yourself in communications with your employees. It means being clear and understandable. Outlaw business- or consultant-speak in your group.

> " *A very experienced communications expert once told me "Effective communications is about reception not transmission". As a manager, your job is to ensure people not only hear the words but understand your message.* "
>
> Jean, Supply Chain Manager, Pharma, UK

Finally, being authentic means … that when you are wrong, you say so. For many people, it's a tough ask to acknowledge that they were wrong. But I believe that you build credibility and trust with your employees if you can acknowledge that you were wrong and demonstrate a willingness to learn.

> " *When you become a manager for the first time, you learn an awful lot about yourself. You don't have all the answers and that's OK. It's a learning journey and it's as much about your development as a person as it is about being a manager.* "
>
> Gene, Regional Director, Pharma, South-East Asia

Show Appreciation and Thanks

Some time ago, I watched the film *Invictus*.[4] One of many things that struck me about the film was the way that Nelson Mandela, portrayed by actor Morgan Freeman, consistently showed his appreciation and thanks to so many different people, from maids and security guards to heads of state, doing so with seeming great ease, humility and sincerity. The sheer number of times he expressed his thanks left me with the impression that this was an accurate depiction of Mandela's own style and grace.

---

[4] *Invictus*, a Clint Eastwood film starring Morgan Freeman and Matt Damon, based on John Carlin's book *Playing the Enemy: Nelson Mandela and the Game that Changed a Nation* (Penguin, 2008).

Saying thanks and showing appreciation, when sincerely and warmly delivered, is about showing gratitude. When received, it is about feeling appreciated. People want to feel appreciated and thanked for their contribution and, even though we sometimes appear to 'brush it off', we are pleased nonetheless when we receive it. Equally, we resent it when we do not receive due appreciation for work well done. We're only human, after all!

> 66 *People want to feel valued and resent it when they are not. After concluding a major project, I typically try to seek out each member of the team to thank them for their contribution to the work. I make sure to focus on the outcome of their efforts and to say that the outcome would not have been achieved without them.* 99
> Kevin, Senior Manager, Government Agency, Ireland

Acknowledging and celebrating team success is a powerful way to thank the individuals involved, while at the same time reinforcing the importance of teamwork and working together. Appreciation replenishes motivation and keeps the momentum going in the team.

Sometimes leaders, in pursuit of excellence, will focus on 'the hole in the doughnut'; and be disappointed that the job was not done to their absolute perfection. We live in a world of normal distribution and not everyone is talented enough or motivated sufficiently to deliver 100% perfection all the time. However, a 90% solution, capable of further improvement next time, still warrants appreciation and recognition. There is no suggestion here that you should show appreciation when it is not warranted: that makes you appear insincere. But when people do a good job, although perhaps not up to your highest standards, they are worthy of some show of appreciation.

*People may forget what you said; they may even forget what you
did; but rarely, if ever, will they forget how you made them feel.*
Maya Angelou, American poet

Whether it is due to the pressure of business or just the culture of
the organisation, we often do not take time to say thanks for a
job well done or an excellent suggestion. I once visited the
headquarters of Milliken & Co., one of the largest privately held
textile and chemical manufacturing companies in the world.
During my visit, I was interested to see several notice boards
dedicated to 'Thanks'. On those boards, staff are encouraged to
write and pin up a thank-you card to express their appreciation
for something an individual, team or other department did for
them. What was most impressive was not only that the boards
were full, but that all the cards were less than a week old.

Accountability

Accountability is perhaps something of an old-fashioned word
these days. It certainly has not been much in evidence in some of
our leaders in politics, public administration, banking
corporations or even an international church in recent decades!
Yet, the concept of accountability was cited by many of the
managers I interviewed as a key determinant of success in career
as well as in life generally. These managers spoke of individuals
who clearly accepted responsibility. They could be relied upon
and trusted to get the job done; they did not blame their
employees for not showing initiative or blame other
departments when things went wrong.

> *Just before I took on my new managerial role, I was made aware of something of a crisis with one of our key customers. Given the standing of the customer and the nature of the problem, I felt I had to go and visit the customer in Chicago on my very first day. To prepare for that, I organised a conference call the day before so that I could be fully briefed on the issues. Based on that call, I felt that the situation was not fantastic but wasn't catastrophic. After my meeting, the customer seemed to calm down and was impressed that I spent my first day on the job in their offices. It bought us some time and goodwill. They felt I was not afraid to take issues right on and was willing to roll up my sleeves. My action also gained me some credibility with my own new team who were with me. They saw me accepting accountability for the project and I was able to hold them equally accountable to meet the commitments we made that day.*
> Anthony, Business Unit VP, Technology Company, US

Really successful departments or teams seem to have a very high level of personal commitment to each other and a willingness to hold each other mutually accountable for results. Your attitude as the new manager is central to creating and sustaining that culture of accountability in your department.

One extreme view can be characterised as "I have 10 people under me". This reflects an attitude of image, status and entitlement, manifested in behaviours of self-importance that greatly inhibit effective listening and reflection. If you indulge your self-importance and inflict it on others, you certainly will not develop any sense of loyalty or commitment from your team.

The opposite view is characterised as "I'm responsible for the performance of a team of 11", reflecting an attitude of accountability and responsibility. The managers I interviewed held the view that the latter, more accountability focused manager, was much more likely to be successful in the long run.

> *An essential early step in making the transition is being honest and straight with people, accepting accountability for the output of the team, showing appreciation and leading by example.*
> Timothy, Manufacturing Operations, Ireland

Western businesses have long pursued paths towards lean manufacturing, total quality management (TQM), autonomous teams and so on. However, for these methodologies to improve organisational efficiency requires something much deeper than the methodology itself; it requires leadership and accountability.

> *Programs will continue to come and go; fads will fade in and fade out, processes will continue evolving and management wizards will keep on multiplying, but the essence of organisational success will only be achieved through the accountable attitudes and actions of individuals.*[5]

In many organisations, personal accountability is an anathema to the culture of the organisation. Some organisations and their managers have made a science as well as an art out of diverting and deflecting responsibility. As a new manager, you need to be able to read and understand your organisation's culture and adjust how best to accept responsibility accordingly. It is difficult, and indeed probably dangerous, to be the only head showing above the parapet. However, you must not capitulate to that culture of responsibility avoidance, somehow believing that you are a victim of your environment. Eventually, you need to look into your own heart and 'to thine own self be true'. If you find yourself in such an accountability-deflecting organisation,

---

[5]   Connors, R., Smith, T. and Hickman, C. (1994). *The Oz Principle: Getting Results Through Individual and Organizational Accountability,* New York: Prentice Hall.

you have to ask yourself the blunt question as to whether this is the right place for you in the long term. Is it a place to really develop your management skills and grow your career?

Leading by Example

When travelling, I regularly met a very senior executive of a large well-known computer company. On medium to short haul flights, he was always seated in economy. His attitude was that he could not tell his staff to cut costs by travelling on economy fares and then proceed to fly business class himself. Leading by example and being consistent in what you do is essential in building trust and commitment on the part of others.

This behaviour is in sharp contrast with a manager who lays off two people in his department in order to cut costs and shows up in the parking lot the following Monday with his shiny new company car. Or a manager who outlaws personal use of the internet during office hours and is found booking family holidays in the middle of the afternoon herself.

> *Leading by example isn't just about the big stuff. Sometimes it's the little things that can make you a bit cynical. A manager I once worked for made big deal about starting his departmental meetings always on time and yet thought nothing about being late for a meeting of a group that you invited him to. He put a high price on his time, but not on ours.*
> Bryan, Director, Management Consulting, Ireland

> *When you become a manager, you must show good example. As a manager, how can I challenge poor performance or high levels of absence or time-keeping if I am guilty myself of the same behaviours?*
> Kevin, Senior Manager, Government Agency, Ireland

A key to building trust and gaining respect is that people know what you stand for and that they see you living to those principles; that you 'walk the talk'. There is no greater source of cynicism, scorn and sarcasm in organisations than leaders who say one thing and immediately do the opposite. After great but hollow speeches, the most typical reaction is likely to be "Yeah, right". If you lead a team that doesn't trust you to 'walk the talk' yourself, you won't be able to engender enthusiasm and commitment for the project and your best people will leave you at the first opportunity.

> *Example is not the main thing in influencing others; it is the only thing.*
> Albert Schweitzer

Just like captains in sport, good managers build an environment of trust and commitment when they lead by example and when they are consistent between what they say and what they do. Back to *Invictus*: when Mandela met François Pienaar, the South African rugby captain, for the first time, he asked him what was his most important principle of leadership, to which Pienaar replied, "I try to lead by example". As you are perhaps aware, South Africa went on to win the Rugby World Cup.

> *If your actions inspire others to dream more, learn more, do more and become more, you are a leader.*
> John Quincy Adams

Conclusion

A corner-stone to being a successful manager is being trusted. To build that trust, you need not only to have sound technical competence but also consistent principles and behaviours. Trust is essentially the product of your technical competence *and* your personal behaviour or characteristics:

$$\text{Trust} = (\text{Technical Competence X Behaviour})$$

Note that the multiplication symbol is deliberate – it is not the sum of the two but the product of the two. This means that a manager with a high level of technical capability who scores low on managerial behaviour will not engender a high level of trust. You need both.

Behaviours around being authentic, accountable, showing appreciation and leading by example are not binary. That is to say that it is not a matter of displaying them or not. They are on a spectrum from low to high. The purpose of raising these behaviours here is to increase an explicit awareness of their importance in leading and managing other people; to encourage you to reflect on them; and hopefully move you along the scale.

CHAPTER 4

CREATING AND
LEADING YOUR TEAM

Nobody doubts the truism that 'the whole is greater than the sum of the parts' or that effective teams almost always will outperform a group of individuals, most especially when the objective requires a variety of complementary skills and behaviours. While it is difficult to definitively measure the bottom-line effect of teamwork, its potential cannot be denied.

In my college days, I used to row (racing shells). Three-quarters way through a 2000 metre race, when your lungs are burning and your muscles are aching with the lactic acid build-up, it is really important for you to believe that the other members of the crew are working just as hard as yourself. If you believe that the others are working that hard, then you find yourself digging even deeper into your reserves. Equally, if you sense some of the others are not working quite so hard, then it is really much more difficult for you, psychologically, to give your best. Effective teamwork requires high levels of trust and support for each other.

Teamwork is one of those concepts like *Quality* that few will argue against. Most managers call for greater teamwork. Some even have nice pictures and rousing mottos on the walls of their departments. However, building teamwork goes way beyond clever mottoes and tee-shirts. Building a team is not about getting people to like each other. It is not even about getting people to be nice to each other. The essential for teamwork is trust. Trying to build a team can be difficult where members have previous poor experience of working with others in the team and levels of trust are low.

> *You have to create the right conditions for a team to work effectively. If you fail to create those conditions, the team won't work. These conditions include trust, fairness and impartiality together with rewards and recognition for a job well done.*
> Kevin, Senior Manager, Government Agency, Ireland

To begin to build effective teamwork in your group, you need to invest time to:

- Clearly communicate the team objective and the sub-elements that make up the objective to help your people understand their roles and interdependencies. Regularly update your team on any changing priorities as part of an ongoing process.

- Build collaboration, cross support and trust. This is obviously much easier said than done. Help team members really get to know each other, to better understand where each other is 'coming from' and to explain their respective and different perspectives. Work with the team to develop *their* set of operating behaviours and norms. Warn against the dangers of 'group think' and encourage team members to argue for their position. Help them to value difference and to understand how difference helps the group. Also agree in advance how differences of opinion will be resolved in order to avoid the team getting bogged down in disagreement. Intel Corporation's slogan "disagree and commit" captures the explicit culture of the way decisions are made in that leading technology company. Early disagreement and debate are welcome but then, after an efficient early review, all the team must unite and be committed to the emerging consensus (even if they still disagree). In essence, team members have the right (and the responsibility) to say their piece early but not the right to block the emerging consensus later. If you end up having to break a 'log-jam' and make a call one way or the other yourself, whenever you can make sure everybody on the team understands your decision and your rationale.

- Related, yet different from the last point, promote an environment where people feel individually and collectively accountable for the team's objective; and where people feel comfortable in constructively addressing and confronting the performance of other members of the team.

- Cross-train individuals so that they can cover for each other and row in to help. People need both the inclination to help *and* the requisite skills to do so.

- Promote respect for different groups, professions and functions. Be sure to outlaw labelling, smart remarks and stereotyping.

- With increased globalisation, it is not unusual to have a geographically dispersed team. In this case be sure to show mutual respect for other nationalities and geographic cultural differences. Also, show some appreciation for significant time differences so that the team member in Australia is not always the person who has to 'dial in' to the conference call at midnight.

- Regularly recognise, reward and where appropriate, celebrate team success. Research shows that the sooner recognition is conveyed, the greater the impact. Make sure that work in teams receives as much recognition as individual performance when it comes to annual performance assessments.

- Finally and most importantly, manage the seeming contradiction or paradox of being able to:
  - Lead your team *while* staying in the background (unless there's an emergency) and
  - Trust your team to make good progress *while* somehow keeping an eye on that progress.

As you begin to build your team, you will find that the traditional role of the manager changes quite dramatically. The evolution towards greater teamwork represents a significant shift from the old command and control model to one of less specific direction; less 'hands on' involvement. Understandably, being less 'hands on' can create a feeling of being less in control and you may find it difficult to achieve the right balance between helping and meddling. As your team develops, it is likely that your role will evolve to being more of a coach and facilitator. As the team develops and you can delegate more to them, you should have more time then to work on more strategic issues and also to focus your efforts on removing blockages to your team's performance – for example, resource issues, politics / interdependencies with other departments, etc.

Giving teams greater autonomy is an evolutionary process. It hardly starts by you pronouncing "Starting next Monday we will have empowerment!" The shift towards greater autonomy has often been described as a journey rather than a destination. Today there is much evidence of work teams managing their own work schedules, shift rosters and vacation plans. Some teams even do their own selection interviewing and recruitment decisions. Some undertake budget setting and control while others go so far as to assess other team members' performance.

The question often is asked about how much decision-making discretion a work team can undertake. The answer always will be governed by the collective skill and expertise of the team on the one hand and, on the other, the key control issues the organisation will never relinquish. It's difficult to imagine a work team in McDonalds in the suburbs of San Diego or Moscow being permitted to change the recipe for the 'Big Mac' at their own discretion.

It's All About Performance

It would be hard to imagine sporting team managers such as Sir Alex Ferguson of Manchester United not being concerned about performance. To achieve success in any sporting endeavour, the manager or coach must be concerned, indeed consumed, by team performance. They must be constantly focused on attracting, developing and motivating talent. Strangely enough, this view of the role of the manager does not always translate into business. Certainly, it translates very well in highly successful organisations but not in every case. In too many situations, managers view their role as no more than minding the budget, attending management meetings and generally supervising an obvious list of tasks to be completed.

Most people want to do good work and not just go through the motions. When people work for a good manager, who respects, challenges and appreciates their work, they will perform at a sustained high level of performance and most of the time actually enjoy the work and the challenge. While different things motivate different people (pay, promotion, recognition, learning opportunities, etc.), there are some basic intrinsic values that motivate most people and build commitment. These include being valued, being treated fairly and appreciated and having a sense that there is a concern for their health and safety.

> *It's really important to me to feel valued. I like it when I'm asked for my opinion and I now try hard to show that same sort of respect by valuing the input and suggestions of my employees.*
> Timothy, Manufacturing Operations, Ireland

> *I love a challenge in my work and I try to challenge*
> *those who work for me. Some welcome that challenge*
> *more than others and I need to be tuned in to who I can*
> *stretch and who I shouldn't stretch too far.*
> Mark, Key Account Manager, Financial Services, US

Research by the Saratoga Institute, a Human Capital division of PricewaterhouseCoopers (PwC) suggests that 50% of work-life satisfaction stems from the relationship an employee has with his/ her boss. A multi-year study of 80,000 managers in 400 companies found that "an employee's relationship with his / her direct boss is more important for retention than company policies such as pay or perks". A third survey of 25,000 employees found that almost 70% of job satisfaction related to the leadership skills of their bosses. All these surveys point to one inescapable reality: the quality of good people management has a direct impact on the operational success of an organisation. It has often been said that people do not leave organisations, they leave poor managers.

> *I've found that while pay and security, especially during*
> *these times, encourage employees to stick around, your*
> *top performers will only stay with you when they are*
> *challenged and where they feel they make a difference.*
> John, Product Development Manager, Technology US

Compliance or Commitment?

A century ago, F.W. Taylor[6] introduced his classic scientific management, measurement and work design propositions, which sought to increase operator productive output though the reduction in variation in work methods, seeking efficiency,

---

6   Taylor, F.W. (1911). *Principles of Scientific Management,* New York: Harper.

predictability and control. Taylor's scientific management was a powerful and successful attempt to understand production efforts. In seeking to maximise predictability of output, scientific management had the effect of removing, even outlawing, discretion by workers: workers became no more than operational cogs in the organisational machine, imagery wonderfully lampooned in the Charlie Chaplin film *Modern Times*.

There is of course another way. Today, successful business leaders are challenging their managers to involve and engage their employees to use their own knowledge, skills, teamwork behaviours and collective intellectual horsepower to improve and drive their business. Achieving superior organisational performance is only possible by tapping the reservoir of talent and releasing the creativity and commitment of your employees. In the past, employees 'checked-in' their creativity on arrival at work. Today, work teams are directly involved in problem-solving and resolving customer issues. We have evolved a long way since Taylor's classic scientific management. Well, some have.

> *There are no short-cuts to creating and sustaining employee involvement and commitment. However, time invested in building commitment will be richly rewarded in terms of performance outcomes.*
> Jean, Supply Chain Manager, Pharma, UK

Conclusion

Strong teamwork environments are characterised by trust, by direct and mature conversation and clarity on the key objectives of the group. Working well, teamwork has the potential to greatly enhance organisational performance by:

- Creating a collective focus and serious commitment to the goal.
- Promoting innovative solutions with diverse viewpoints and experience.
- Generating a greater sense of involvement and engagement.
- Promoting a greater sense of mutual accountability towards the goal.

Sporting managers are consumed by performance in the stadium. As a new manager in business, you too must be concerned about the performance of your team. Only in engaging the involvement and commitment of your team and releasing their collective creativity will you, as a manager, grow and enhance your own performance and continued career growth.

PART 2

A TOOL KIT OF PEOPLE MANAGEMENT SKILLS

CHAPTER 5

MANAGING THROUGH INFLUENCE

Perhaps one of the biggest surprises in store for new managers is how little formal power and authority you actually have in trying to get things done. An understandable error is to allocate way too much of your time to the obvious chain of command – that is, to your employees and to a lesser extent, your boss. New managers do not spend nearly enough time with peer support organisations or their internal customers.

In most organisations, there is a very high degree of interdependency between departments and groups and your success as a new manager depends very much on your capacity to influence and persuade people outside of your direct chain of command. Building relationships and creating supportive alliances and networks both inside and outside your organisation are essential to your success. Therefore it is important:

- To understand what these interdependencies are.
- To understand who the key players are
- To build influence and alliances with them.

At first glance, this may sound rather political and possibly even manipulative but the reality is that you and your department are likely to be part of a much bigger system – a cog in a bigger machine – and influence, persuasion, cooperation and win-win negotiation are the lubricants that allow that machine to work.

It may seem to you that as a new manager, you probably will not have to manage significant change initiatives straight away and as a consequence do not need to unduly concern yourself about building trust and influence. The reality is that you send out signals about yourself in your new role from the very start and people will form views about you and your style from the very beginning.

Trust and Reciprocity

A key foundation for influence is trust. Spend time with your key stakeholders, occasionally in their office, to begin to build a firm relationship based on mutual trust and reciprocity. Bear in mind that people judge you on your actions, not your intentions. Most often you build trust by:

- By being reliable and doing what you said you would do.
- Helping people understand 'where you are coming from' and your agenda.
- Demonstrating acceptance of accountability (**Chapter 3**).
- Being consistent in your principles and your behaviour.
- Attending and engaging in meetings you said you would attend.
- Addressing and confronting issues, based on the issue, not the personality.

In simple terms, trust and reciprocity are about developing a reliable supportive 'give-and-take' relationship between you and your team and those with whom you have mutual interfaces.

Given the interdependencies involved, you need to identify the key stakeholders, together with their levels of organisational power and influence regarding your objectives and initiatives. From those stakeholders, you need to be able to identify your supporters, those likely to resist and the 'swing voters'. Get to know these people and, just as importantly, let them get to know you. You should not wait until you have a grand plan to roll out before you talk to the stakeholders. Spend time with them to really get to know their issues and concerns. Understand the key mutual interfaces that you have and where you need to support and cooperate with each other.

> " *It's very time-consuming to build a network of relationships but it is essential that you take the time to do it. Try to understand the interests and agendas of others and help them to understand 'where you are coming from'. Be pro-active sharing information both good and bad news.* "
> Gene, Regional Director, Pharma, South-East Asia

Conclusion

John Kotter,[7] a leading expert on leadership and change, urges managers to form a 'powerful coalition' with their boss and all key stakeholders in managing change. In embarking on change, it is essential that you influence and persuade these key players and get them on-side with your objectives, using their organisational power and resources to help and support you as you undertake the change effort.

---

[7]   Kotter, J. (1996). *Leading Change*, Boston: Harvard Business School Press.

CHAPTER 6

MANAGING YOURSELF

There is little return in trying to improve your skills in managing others, if you cannot manage yourself and your own effectiveness. You will not win much credibility as a manager of others if they see you having difficulty managing yourself.

Do you occasionally go home at the end of the day feeling frustrated that you were unable to complete a set of tasks you set for yourself at the beginning of the day because you got caught up by busywork? Back-to-back meetings and responding to urgent calls easily conspire to eat up that most precious commodity, your time. Clearly, there are days when it just cannot be helped but if it becomes the norm then you have to step back and seriously examine how effectively you use your time and how well you are delegating responsibilities and tasks to other members of your team.

Effective Use of Time

There is a long list of culprits that that have the potential to steal your time. These include:

- Not sticking to priorities.
- Poor planning.
- Insufficient delegation.
- Procrastination.
- Telephone interruptions and drop-in visitors.
- Poorly-run meetings.

- E-mail and the web, the worst culprits.

Time is a resource and, unlike some other resources, time wasted today cannot be recaptured tomorrow. Take time out to plan. Tackle important priority items first. Avoid the temptation to drop what you are doing to respond to e-mails. Set a designated time of the day to deal with e-mail traffic. Delegate effectively and develop others. And learn to say "No".

> " *My life had become just a series of back-to-back meetings. There was no time available to really plan and get things done. Because things were so bad, I requested my managerial colleagues not to convene meetings before 10.30 in the morning – to which they agreed. This non-meeting window of time gave me the predictable quality time I needed to plan and execute my really important work.* "
> Jean, Supply Chain Manager, Pharma, UK

This is not just about 'time management'; it is about being disciplined and focused on the truly vital few goals that make the difference. Stephen Covey usefully distinguishes between activities that are urgent and activities that are important.[8] Urgent and important are not the same thing: just because something is urgent doesn't necessarily mean it is important. Too often we feel compelled to rush to address matters that are urgent or seem to be urgent at the expense of dealing with matters that are important.

The irony is that urgent work is often the result of a larger broken system and thus the urgency to fix problems that are symptoms of the system robs us of the time to complete a more

---

[8]   Covey, S. (2004). *The Seven Habits of Effective People*, New York: The Free Press.

complete analysis that would allow us to fix the larger broken system.

> *There was a time when we were so busy responding to a customer return that we failed to notice that this was the fifth return in a month and if we'd only stopped to think about it, we'd have realised that this was the same product problem and that what we needed was a full root-cause analysis to understand why the product was failing in the field and to put a remedial fix in place.*
> Edward, Manufacturing Operations Director, Ireland

You have limited time resources and you need to decide where that time is best invested for greatest return. It is a matter of making choices. Use the 'Is this the best use of my time right now?' test. This explicit questioning in your mind offers you a way to quickly and confidently reduce superfluous demands and allows you to focus on what you assess to be really important.

Making a 'To Do' list is always helpful but do remember that not all items on that list are born equally. It is essential that you distinguish between the important items and the urgent ones, making sure you carve out time for the important ones. If you have several important or A items, then you need to prioritise which is the most important. Your A priorities should be Covey's 'important' tasks. Make sure to work on your A tasks before your B tasks and really question the necessity to complete C items.

Procrastination is one of the major reasons for not getting on with important work. This can be due to a sense of being overwhelmed with the scale of the project, to the point that you do not quite know where to begin. The solution to being overwhelmed may be contained in the hoary question: "How do you eat an elephant? Answer: In small bites!" Instead of looking for the distraction of urgent tasks elsewhere, do something, anything that will advance your project. See if you can start to break the project down into more manageable tasks. Perhaps pull together a short meeting of interested parties to generate some ideas to advance the project.

Saying "No" to requests was dealt with from a different perspective in **Chapter 3** (*Being Authentic*). We often struggle with saying "No" because we may want an 'obliging person' image; or we may be afraid of offending people; or there may be an organisational culture that does not let us say "No"; or perhaps we just do not have our priorities clear. The harsh reality however is that if you do not say "No", you will not have time for your own important work. Approaches for saying "No" include indicating an interest in the issue but explaining your priorities. You also could negotiate – explain that you cannot take on the task now but could later, or offer another report or resource that might meet 75% of the person's needs.

Having advocated the need to say "No" sometimes, it must be stressed that organisations do need a culture of teamwork and mutual support. Therefore, it is really important to be able to balance being supportive while at the same time being able to manage your own *important* goals:

- Organisations with a strong 'It's not my job' mentality are never going to achieve high performance; also typically they are not usually nice places to work.
- Equally, organisations with everyone being so helpful but thereby not getting their important work done will not achieve high performance either.

It is a matter of achieving balance and being comfortable with the paradox of mutual support while managing your own important work.

Delegation

When you delegate effectively, you get the time to plan and focus on your important goals. You now need to focus less on individual assignments and more on managing and leading. As was pointed out in **Chapter 1**, your promotion into management means that you have had to swop your musical instrument for a conductor's baton.

It is not at all unusual for a newly promoted manager to hesitate in delegating assignments that he or she once did themself. This was work they were obviously good at and were well recognised for. It can be very difficult to hand over choice assignments to others and no longer be able to enjoy the gratification and sense of achievement once the assignment is completed.

As with any goal-setting process, it is important to clarify clear expectations of performance for any delegated assignment. Even very experienced employees perform poorly if they do not have clear directions and standards of performance to deliver to. In simple terms, be clear about the task; check that the employee has the same understanding; keep an eye on progress but do not interfere unnecessarily. Finally, you need to accept responsibility for the outcome if it does not work out well, while at the same time giving full credit to the employee if it does.

Wherever possible, assign whole projects rather than parts of projects to individuals or groups. In this way, they will more likely develop a greater 'total system' solution, feel a greater sense of accountability and enjoy a greater sense of achievement once completed. Whole projects also facilitate clearer assessment of performance when the project is completed.

Giving a plum assignment to one or more of your employees is an important form of reward and recognition. However, in giving the assignment to one employee, take time to explain to the others why you have chosen the employee you are giving it to.

As with any group, you will have some employees who are more capable and motivated than others. Given that situation, there is a natural temptation to delegate key assignments to those who you know are most reliable and competent. The obvious drawbacks with this approach are that you will never know whether others in the group also are capable and willing to take on such an assignment. These untested employees will not have the same development opportunities and will miss out on the chance to prove themselves to you. If you regularly turn to the same small number of tried and trusted employees, do not be surprised that the others will seek to exercise their potential and learning elsewhere. Another reason to share the assignments is to balance and distribute the workload across all your employees in a fair and equitable way.

> *If you don't trust someone to do a task, then don't delegate it to them and try to micro-manage it. That's hell for the employee and hell for you. You'll end up basically doing their job and, as a consequence, probably not doing your own job.*
> Gene, Regional Director, Pharma, South-East Asia

You should agree a process for regular review and updates. There is a fine line between continuous checking and looking over the shoulder of the individual or team and cutting them loose and appearing to take little or no interest. The level of ongoing review should be influenced by the importance of the assignment, together with the capability and motivation of the individual or team.

There can be a very fine line between delegation and abdication. You may delegate tasks and projects but you cannot delegate accountability. Good managers and leaders delegate effectively but understand that the 'buck stops with me'.

> *I had a senior manager one time who delegated a very important project to us. We couldn't agree on a final recommendation and try as we might, we just couldn't engage with him. This went on for ages and he just wouldn't make a decision one way or the other. So this important project just languished there and none of us covered ourselves in glory.*
> Jean, Supply Chain Manager, Pharma, UK

Effective delegation offers huge advantages. Advantages to you as you create space and time to manage and lead and advantages to your employees who feel they are doing more interesting work and learning.

Conclusion

Managing other people can be a challenge. However, that challenge is all the greater when your employees see you having difficulty managing yourself. Your time resource is finite so it is essential for you to be disciplined to keep your focus on your truly important goals – the vital few that will make the difference. Delegate where you can and avoid procrastination on major projects.

> *It is absurd that a man should rule others, who cannot rule himself.*
> Latin maxim

CHAPTER 7

ADDRESSING PERFORMANCE AND GIVING FEEDBACK

Some years ago, I was training a group of managers in performance management. Part of the programme included practice sessions recorded on video. One manager, in an attempt to put his employee at ease, opened with the line "I hope this won't be too painful". Too painful for whom?

I have been talking to groups of managers about performance management for a very long time now. Each time I start such a discussion or training session, I usually ask the group for a show of hands from those who like doing performance appraisals. In all my years, I have rarely seen a hand raised. Not only do these managers not like doing performance appraisals, many acknowledge that these appraisals are the most dreaded task in their calendar, second only to root canal work. Too often these annual appraisal procedures become ritualistic rain dances with shallow discussions and both parties colluding to meet the prescribed administrative procedure.

There is a lot of rhetoric around the importance of performance management. Proliferations of text books and management journals tell us that objective and candid feedback is essential for organisational improvement and success. Yet, when it comes to completing performance appraisals and giving feedback, managers look for all sorts of reasons to procrastinate or indeed try to avoid doing it altogether.

One of the reasons why managers do not like doing performance appraisals is because they see performance as something that they have to deal with on a formal procedural basis once a year. This annual attempt leaves both the appraiser and appraisee conflicted in roles and relationships, as 364 days of the year the manager is a colleague and then, on the 365th day, judge and jury!

Many of us immediately put up our guard when we hear the words "I'd like to give you some feedback". That is a fairly normal and understandable reaction when the feedback is perceived as *judgement*, and especially when such feedback is infrequent and poorly delivered. Good managers take time out of their busy schedules to give feedback on a very regular basis as part of their day-to-day relationship. It would be very hard to imagine a sports coach refraining from giving direct and 'real-time' feedback to their athletes before, during and after a performance. Imagine Sir Alex Ferguson, Manchester United's manager, waiting until the annual performance appraisal event each January before giving squad members feedback!

Whether it is on the sports pitch or in the office, good managers take time to talk regularly to their employees, discuss the status of specific goals and priorities and give feedback both positive and areas for improvement. When such discussions happen with regularity, the 'annual appraisal' becomes nothing more than a summary of discussions that have taken place throughout the year and year-end surprises are avoided. I also contend that, when feedback is accompanied with some coaching, your employee is more likely to be open and receptive to feedback. Whether it is in sports or in the office, feedback is an essential element in the learning and development process.

However, human nature means there will always be the potential for some level of conflict between your feedback and your employees' wish for feedback consistent with their self-image and hoped-for rewards. Their personal development requires openness on their part to your feedback and coaching. They need to be willing to lower their defences, fully consider your view of their performance and be open to exploring how they might best improve their performance. However, this openness may not always serve an individual's objective of gaining pay increases, bonuses and promotions when these are in short supply. Nonetheless, I still contend that you are better off talking about performance on a regular basis than waiting for the 'dreaded annual event'.

> *I find that it is much easier to give feedback very soon after an event or project completion. If I act quickly, I find it much easier to be specific with my feedback. If I wait, I can easily forget to do it, whether it was positive or corrective feedback. If someone is starting to drift off satisfactory performance, be sure to tell them straight away and help them to address it, rather than it becoming a bigger problem later on.*
> Gene, Regional Director, Pharma, South-East Asia

It is really hard to measure an employee against their goals if the goals are ambiguous in the first place. Really effective goals are cascaded down from key organisational goals or key performance indicators (KPIs), through departmental goals to team and individual performance goals. Effective (SMART) goals are: specific, measurable, achievable, rated in priority and time-bound. Careful goal-setting with regular reviews recognises the reality that goals or priorities set a year ago are likely to have changed in the meantime, so regular updates are needed to acknowledge and agree changing goals and priorities.

'People are our most important asset' rings rather hollow when you look generally at the performance management experience in many organisations. There is good news however. In their extensive research into performance management, Mohrman and his colleagues at the Centre for Effective Organizations found that done well, feedback does make a difference: "The higher the quality of the appraisal process, the more the appraisal event results in performance improvement and better working relations between the subordinate and the supervisor".[9]

Giving Feedback

Focus on what your employee needs to hear, not on what you need to say.

Giving vent to your frustration is not feedback. Dealing with poor employee performance or behaviour of course can be frustrating. The key is to deal with your frustration. Count up to 10; bite your tongue if you have to; but wait to give feedback until you are reasonably calm and can keep your focus on the performance issue and not the person.

Sarcastic comments have no place in a leader's lexicon. Such destructive comments, with or without intention, serve no purpose but to put people down, belittle them in front of others or to assert ourselves as their superior. They not only disparage the employee, but also can make their colleagues uncomfortable and ill-at-ease. Continuous sarcasm tends to create a corrosive climate that people want to escape from at the earliest opportunity. Some managers defend this practice suggesting that they are only 'kidding' – no kidding.

Tips for giving feedback include:

---

[9]   Mohrman, A. (1990). *Performance Appraisal Research at the Centre for Effective Organizations*, Technical report T 90-7 (169), Los Angeles: University of Southern California.

- **Give timely feedback:** Feedback is most effective when delivered 'real-time'. By taking time out from your schedule, you demonstrate that it is important. It also is much easier for you and your employee to recall the issue. If you wait until the annual appraisal procedure then it is more difficult to give feedback to an employee who does not remember, or says that they do not remember. Giving regular feedback avoids presenting your employees with 'surprises' at the annual appraisal procedure.

- **Be specific:** Do not generalise. Be clear and specific. Avoid "You're not a good team player" or "I don't think you're pulling your weight". Try to be clear and specific and avoid being oblique, hoping your employee picks up the message or hint. Offer them concrete examples of what you observed and what behaviour you want them to change or skill you want them to improve.

- **Focus on the future, not the past:** Learn from the past but your primary focus should be on improving in the future. Try to keep the keep the focus on 'where we go from here'. Create and agree a plan of action and agree a process for regular review and coaching.

- **Explain the impact:** Explain the effect your employee's performance or behaviour is having. Explain why the issue is important to you, their team, and the customer. Describe the knock-on effect of their behaviour or lack of skill.

- **Put into context:** 'Size' the issue for your employee. Make sure they understand whether this is a serious problem or a minor correction, a major achievement or nice effort.

- **Find the right setting:** Find some place private to give corrective feedback. Your employee is much more likely to hear your feedback if you do it in private. If you do it in public, the employee typically is more concerned about dealing with their embarrassment than listening to what you are saying. On the other hand, find a public place to give praise and recognition for a job well done. Praising people in public also lets your other employees know that you recognize and appreciate superior performance. Be sure to be authentic.

- **Speak for yourself:** Should you receive feedback about one of your employees, satisfy yourself about the situation. Do not act as spokesperson for someone else. Avoid "They aren't pleased ..." Satisfy yourself that there is an issue. If there is, deal with it!

- **Focus on the vital few:** If you have several issues to deal with, focus on the vital few. Do not overload your employee with lots of feedback (think of the ineffective golf coach who asks you to remember 15 things during your swing!). Give the recipient a chance to absorb.

- **Stop talking and start listening:** Give your employee the chance to offer their perspective. The problem you started out to address may be only a symptom of a different issue. Be willing to listen and explore further with your employee.

- **Check-in to see if they have reflected on the discussion:** If the issue is sufficiently important then check in with the employee a few days afterwards to see if they had reflected on the matter.

When to Give Feedback

Regularly scheduled meetings to discuss performance and changing priorities afford you the opportunity to give feedback and coach your employees in an atmosphere that seems less judgmental than the annual performance appraisal procedure. However, you should not confine yourself only to those scheduled meetings.

Consider offering feedback when:

- **Good work has been completed:** At the end of a successful project, the completion of an important sale or on receiving positive feedback from a client. Positive and authentic feedback is not given often enough and yet its benefits can be great.
- **An employee is showing high potential and you want to actively encourage their continued development:** A 'keep up the good work' conversation.
- **A problem cannot be ignored:** When the person's performance or behaviour is having a negative impact on the organisation or where they are resisting change.

Immediate feedback, however, might not be a good idea when:

- You do not have all the facts and need to gather further information before deciding on action to be taken.
- Where the situation has become somewhat heated and you and others may need some time to calm down before dealing with the situation.

Coaching

In the ever-flatter, faster-changing organisations of today, your job as a manager gets more demanding by the day. You have a wide range of responsibilities to carry out and you are increasingly expected to fulfil even broader roles in relation to people management and development without dropping any existing responsibilities.

Coaching can take many forms. There are athletics coaches, executive coaches, even 'life' coaches. What I am referring to in this context of management is more about your *style* of managing your department or leading your team. It is not so much something extra that you have to do, but rather more about *how* you manage. A coaching style of managing does not suggest constant coaching sessions but more about a helpful style of day-to-day managing. Coaching at this level is about offering advice and suggestions to your employee about their approach to a new project or their preparation for an upcoming important presentation. At another level, it is about taking time to address an employee behaviour issue. Much of this can and should happen in a 'real-time' interactive way and not necessarily in a more formal meeting setting.

Line managers point to time constraints as a serious barrier to achieving a coaching style of managing. However, if your ultimate aim is performance improvement of your team, then an investment in modulating your management style to include regular, balanced, positive, constructive and encouraging guidance and coaching should be a significant contributor towards achieving performance improvement.

Addressing Poor Performance

Occasionally, despite helpful feedback and coaching, there is an emerging reality that your employee's performance or behaviour is not improving and that you need to address the situation with greater formality than before. Hoping the problem will go away on its own is just wishful thinking. There is a real danger that, by avoiding giving your employee feedback, you can create a culture of the *status quo* of poor performance, not just for that employee but for the other employees in the group.

Many larger organisations have Human Resources departments with clearly defined disciplinary procedures, which should be followed very carefully. While these procedures differ in detail from organisation to organisation and substantially from country to country, the following is a useful generic approach:

- Mindful of the advice about giving feedback above, address the performance / behaviour issue directly with your employee. Be very specific on the issue to be resolved and set clear performance standards to be met. You also should explain that you have now moved from a general coaching approach and into a disciplinary process. Explain the steps of your disciplinary procedure. Develop a performance improvement plan with your employee. Immediately afterwards, document the essential details of your meeting and give your employee a copy, together with a copy of the improvement plan and your organisation's disciplinary procedure.

- Give time to improve. Three months might be typical but ensure compliance with your organisation's disciplinary procedure. Monitor performance closely during that time and provide feedback.

- If your employee's performance or behaviour does not improve in your specified time-frame at a level defined in the performance improvement plan, then you should again have a formal meeting with your employee. Ensure all procedural steps are adhered to, including the right of your employee to be accompanied. You should advise the employee that standards were not achieved and explain that you have now moved to the next step of your disciplinary procedure. It is essential that you clearly explain to your employee the consequences of failure to improve, which may include dismissal. Again, everything should be documented, with a copy given to your employee. You should also advise your employee that they have the right to access an appeal procedure.

- If, after all the appropriate disciplinary steps, performance / behaviour does not improve, you should recommend that your employee should be dismissed, as long as:

o You are satisfied that you have fully complied with the disciplinary procedure.

o You have demonstrated to your HR department and your manager that all procedures have been complied with

Giving Feedback – or Are You Bullying?

It is possible that your employee may respond to your feedback and disciplinary steps by charging you with bullying and harassment. Sometimes, sadly, the prospect of such a charge of harassment scares some managers from following through on performance management and disciplinary procedures. Most company procedures and 'respect at work' policies state that managers have both a right and a duty to manage. The stoutest defences to a claim of harassment and / or wrongful termination of employment are clear standards of performance and a well-documented adherence to procedures.

Conclusion

Giving regular feedback and coaching encourages your employees to higher levels of performance; makes them feel recognized for their efforts; and is an important element in developing and retaining them. Managing performance should really be about bringing *performance* into sharper and more regular focus. An organisation with a culture characterised by regular and open feedback, balanced with positive and constructive messages, tends to have employees who feel committed, valued and willing to learn and change.

CHAPTER 8

MANAGING TO LISTEN

... AND LISTENING TO MANAGE

In his best-selling book *The Seven Habits of Highly Effective People*, Stephen Covey recommends that you "seek first to understand, then to be understood". Good doctors spend time carefully listening to their patient for clues that will help them with their diagnosis. This careful listening is supplemented with vigilant enquiry, probing for additional information and further clues. Just as with good doctors, active listening and enquiry for understanding is an essential skill for managers.

Active Listening

Careful listening and effective enquiry sometimes is referred to as 'active listening'. Active listening means just that: you listen and enquire carefully so that you not only hear the words but also you understand what the person is telling you. Not all of your employees and colleagues are likely to be gifted communicators so it is important that you get to the bottom of what is being said.

On the face of it, it may seem rather obvious: people talk and you listen. Unfortunately, it is really not that simple at all. Active listening means that you listen carefully to really understand what is being said. By listening and enquiring carefully, you seek out what people mean, not just what they say. Listen carefully and enquire fully to differentiate between facts, opinions and agendas. Probe with words like *why, when, how*.

When engaged in diagnosis, ask *why* several times as you peel away outer layers of the onion to identify the root cause.

> *I heard it said that we are born with two ears and one mouth and that we should apply the same ratio between listening and talking: listen twice as much as you talk. Some managers I've watched over the years just love the sound of their own voice. But the really excellent managers I've observed are very good listeners.*
> Jean, Supply Chain Manager, Pharma, UK

Be very careful of being influenced unduly by whether you like the person delivering the message or whether you like the message being delivered. As objectively and as carefully as you can, evaluate the information and enquire further if you feel you do not fully understand the situation being explained.

> *It is very important not to 'shoot the messenger'. If you react poorly to bad news being delivered then don't be surprised if people stop coming to give you news or information in the future; information that might be essential to the performance of you and your team.*
> Timothy, Manufacturing Operations, Ireland

Active listening is about searching for understanding and clarity. Once you think you understand the message, test that you do by paraphrasing or summarising what you believe you heard "So, what you are telling me is …?"

Active listening goes beyond using our ears; we should also listen with our eyes. Sometimes the words of a message are saying one thing while the person's facial expression or mannerisms are saying something quite different. Be prepared to question your employee by saying something like "You don't seem to be very happy about that?" If in giving an instruction to your employee, you ask them if they understand the instruction and they reply that they do but their 'body language' seems to say otherwise, then enquire further to check as to whether they really do understand the instruction. Active listening is about using our ears, our eyes, our mouth when appropriate and our brain all the time!

There is of course a danger that your employee may equate your attentive listening with your agreement. Just by listening carefully to your employee(s) does not mean that you agree or that you are making some kind of commitment. Consequently, to avoid a misunderstanding of what is actually being agreed, as distinct from what has been discussed, it is helpful to summarise what you heard and indicate what you plan to do about it. What you plan to do about it might be as little as "I'm going to chat with a few more people about this and think about it some more".

> *You need to be really careful in conversations with some people. Either through their deliberate effort to position you or just their misplaced optimism, the employee thinks that you have made a commitment to them. It's a really good idea to tell the employee what, if anything, you intend to do about it.*
> Bryan, Director, Management Consulting, Ireland

Effective Dialogue

When asked by your 7-year old "What do you do at work?", it is often hard to do more than explain limply that you have meetings and you talk to people.

That description is not far from the truth. That is what managers do. While we could talk about all the important decisions we make every day, the reality is that managers mostly engage in dialogue to seek information and updates, give feedback and coaching, address performance issues and seek to resolve conflicts.

Therefore, a key skill for managers is the art of effective conversation. We all have different perspectives, different levels of experience, and different levels of ambition and it is only through conversation and dialogue that we can begin to understand other perspectives and possibilities. Once people really understand what others are saying, they are usually better able to work together. It does not mean that you have to agree on everything but if you at least understand where the other person is coming from, there is likely to be greater levels of respect and trust.

When things 'blow-up' between people, as they inevitably do sometimes, it is usually because we have stopped listening to each other.

Meetings

One of my favourite moments in the management training video *Meetings, Bloody Meetings* was when the John Cleese character's wife asked him why he held Wednesday Meetings, and he replied in a most frustrated and dismissive manner that it was "because it was Wednesday! We always have our meeting on Wednesday!" Lots of meetings are held just because they are on the meeting schedule. And so managers often scramble at the last moment to cobble together an agenda. The management press has a rich vein of books on the topic of effective meetings. All I want to address here is meetings in the context of listening and dialogue.

As a new manager, it is likely that you will need to hold team meetings. Since lots of staff hours can be wasted by ineffective meetings, it is essential that you manage meetings efficiently. Efficient in this context does not mean that the meeting finishes on time. Sadly, too often dialogue at meetings is one-sided with participants taking their lead from the leader, with participants saying what they are supposed to, barely perceptible nods on action plans and allocated assignments. It is only afterwards that there is any discussion and commentary, often taking place later in smaller groups in the coffee dock or rest-rooms!

Efficient meeting are those that discuss and debate the merits of a proposal and arrive at a clear consensus with participants feeling they had an opportunity to contribute, contributed as best they could, and focused on the proposal not personalities. It is up to you as the meeting leader to create and develop a climate where people actively listen to each other and confront differences of opinion in an open and constructive manner.

From the beginning, establish 'ground rules':

- Everyone understands the objective of the meeting and has a copy of the agenda well in advance. Distinguish between items for information, items for discussion and items for decision.

- Everyone respects each other's time and ensures that they show up on time for the meeting. Make punctuality an expected behaviour.

- If you commit to keeping the meeting short and efficient, then it is reasonable to ask people to put their mobile phones on silent and not take calls or deal with e-mails during the meeting.

- Everyone has a collective responsibility to keep each other on topic.

- Everyone contributes to key discussions. If you feel the meeting is being dominated by some participants, invite others into the debate: "Mike, you've been quiet on this topic so far, what do you think?"

- "The brain can only absorb what the seat of the pants can endure". Balance your meetings to be as short as possible with enough time to address the issues properly.

- Decisions are confirmed and key points briefly summarised. Key decisions, accountabilities and time-frames are minuted and circulated immediately after the meeting. Review the open action items early on in the next meeting. Hold people accountable.

E-mail May Be Communications – But Is It Listening?

E-mail has revolutionised how people communicate with each other. However, while e-mail offers extraordinary speed and cost advantages, it also has the potential to impact negatively on the quality of effective communications and teamwork. Sadly, e-mail is often the *de rigueur* procedure of communicating between what is in effect not a team but rather a collection of individuals or departmental silos.

> *I have seen situations both in business settings and in voluntary organisation committees where e-mail messages caused serious fractures in relationships or reinforced earlier rifts. These fractures can be caused by content, 'tone' of the message or indeed the fact that others are copied.*
> Mark, Key Account Manager, Financial Services, US

Probably the most counterproductive use of e-mail is in continuous debate backwards and forwards between the protagonists on both side of an argument. It is often the case that this succession of messages is not the exchange of opinions, but merely an opportunity to pontificate endlessly with no capacity or intention to conclude the debate or to offer a process to resolve the conflict. Far from resolving issues and disputes, these endless e-mail chains have the capacity both to polarize positions and further entrench people in their chosen positions.

> *Endless 'pinging' of e-mails backwards and forwards is not just a symptom of poor teamwork. I would assert that it is also a symptom of a leadership vacuum. You need to confront such unproductive practices of endless debate and create an environment and processes where differing views can be aired and discussed face-to-face.*
> Jessica, Department Manager, Financial Services, UK

Conclusion

Since you do not have a whole lot of time to spend with each employee, you need to find the right balance: enough time and skilled listening and enquiry to understand what is going on and not so much that little else is achieved.

CHAPTER 9

SELECTING GOOD PERFORMERS

Managers have no greater opportunity to impact on the performance of their team than the opportunity to choose who joins their team.

> *Successful managers surround themselves with the best people they can find. Making a bad hiring decision will kill you.*
> Marcus, VP Operations, US

Recruitment and selection processes vary greatly from one organisation to another. During the period 1990 to 1995, Sun Microsystems was one of the fastest growing US companies with annual growth rates of up to 100%. Filling vacancies to fuel that growth was an extraordinary challenge. Despite the urgent pressures to hire people, Sun's selection process was highly labour-intensive and time-consuming. Candidates were invited back for further selection interviews three or four times with an array of different people before job offers were extended. Virtually every person who interviews at Google talks to at least four interviewers from management and potential colleagues. Toyota (USA) screened 50,000 applications for 3,000 factory jobs for its new plant in Georgetown, Kentucky. This selection process included tests on general knowledge, aptitude tests, interpersonal skills assessment, hands-on manual dexterity tests, an extensive personal interview and a medical examination.

Whether you work in a large organisation with many sophisticated selection processes, or where the Human

Resources Department has done some preliminary screening before handing the candidate over to you, the ultimate decision in many organisations to hire someone for your department rests with you as the manager.

Many organisations' annual reports and glossy recruitment brochures proclaim that "people are our most important resource". Yet lots of managers in those same organisations pay scant attention to adequate planning and preparation before making some of their most important decisions – selecting their employees. The purchase of a piece of capital equipment costing $1 million is likely to be subject to thorough financial analysis, including pay-back period analysis and cost / benefit analysis. However, a selection decision on a new employee on a salary of $70k plus benefits, who stays in employment for 25 years, is likely to cost twice as much as that piece of capital equipment. However, often the candidate selection criteria are unclear and the actual selection decision is based on intuition and gut-feel. The selection process is rarely as rigorous as it should be, given the stakes involved.

> " *Rushing through a selection interview because you are busy and as a consequence, you make a poor selection decision, the result will certainly keep you busy into the future as you try to address the new employee's performance because of the rushed selection decision you made.* "
> Mark, Key Account Manager, Financial Services, US

A poor selection decision will result in you spending a disproportionate of your time managing your employee, addressing performance issues. Far from being able to delegate responsibilities to this individual, you will end up having to monitor all of their work. Worse than that, a really poor hiring decision may result in disruption and disharmony among the rest of your team.

> *I once interviewed and hired an employee the morning after a big party. I was definitely not at my best. Ten years on, he is still the bane of our lives. I should have postponed the interview.*
> Jean, Supply Chain Manager, Pharma, UK

This is certainly one area where *prevention* (meaning thoughtful clarity on criteria and effective enquiry through the interview) is much better than months, if not years, of attempts at *cure*.

Some managers seem to feel that a mistake in a selection decision has little real cost attached because the employee's employment can be terminated. Viewed narrowly, a mistake in a selection decision might be costed as the sum of severance pay (which, in some countries, might amount to two years' pay) and the recruitment agency fees to find a replacement (often 15% to 20% of annual pay). The reality, however, is very different. Many poorly selected employees stick around for a very long time as some managers can be quite creative in avoiding dealing with sub-standard performance. And in some protected environments, such as the civil service in some countries, there is no termination of employment.

Costs of poor selection that typically go unmeasured include:

- The employee's lower level of productivity while he / she was employed.
- Your own lower level of productivity since you cannot delegate.
- The cost of poor decisions by the employee.
- The cost of training a replacement.
- Lower productivity by subordinates of the employee.

- The potential reputational damage of becoming a 'hire and fire' manager – or, worse, organisation.

Some estimates of these indirect costs can be as much as a multiple of five to 10 times the direct cost (severance plus replacement recruitment).

Errors in Selection

New managers often make simple mistakes in selecting staff, sometimes with disastrous consequences. Common errors include:

- Not explicitly defining the job and the essential requirements.
- Poor interview planning.
- Interview focus too narrow.
- Poor questioning technique.

Not Explicitly Defining the Job and the Essential Requirements

It is very important that you clearly define the role and nature of the job to be filled together with the essential knowledge, skills and behaviours necessary to be successful in that job. This process has less to do with HR bureaucracy (as you might see it) and more to do with clarifying exactly what you are searching for. You need to be clear in answering the question: what knowledge, skills and behaviours are essential and without which, the candidate will *not* be successful in the job?

> Before you start looking, it's vital that you know exactly what you're looking for! I am clear that I want people who can show some flexible thinking and who are open to change. For some jobs I'm looking for some creativity. In all cases, I'm looking for people who are enthusiastic – about their work and about themselves.
> **Gene, Regional Director, Pharma, South-East Asia**

A common mistake in employment selection is where the manager selects the best candidate, although they still may not have all the essential knowledge, skills and behaviours necessary to be successful in the vacancy. Essential knowledge, skills and behaviours are not the same as 'desired' or wished for. The *essential* competencies are those vital few competencies without which, the candidate will not be successful in the job.

There is a lot of responsibility on your shoulders in selecting the right candidate not just from your organisational perspective but also for the candidate's benefit. You do no favours for a candidate in selecting them, getting them to leave their current employment, and bringing them on-board your organisation if they do not have the essential competencies and end up being unsuccessful. Making job offers while not being crystal clear about the essential competencies to be successful can be irresponsible to all concerned.

Poor Interview Planning

Good interviewers, whether for an employment interview or a radio chat show, prepare well in advance. Sadly however, I have observed managers, when advised that their candidate was in Reception waiting for their interview, quickly glancing over the candidate's CV / résumé, too often for the first time.

The purpose of the interview is for the interviewer to systematically collect information, evidence and clues about the candidate's ability to perform satisfactorily in the areas that are considered *essential* competencies. Good planning facilitates a systematic collection of important information central to making a sound selection decision. It is unlikely that, as a relatively new manager, you will be skilled in conducting an employment interview. Given that, it is more important than ever that you plan and prepare well in advance. It also makes sense to enrol the help and support of a more experienced colleague to partner with you in the interview process. Your Human Resources Department also should be of help and support to you through the process.

Interview Focus Too Narrow

In my experience, I have found some managers focus very narrowly on the candidate's education and experience. While these are obvious areas for exploration, the interview needs to seek out clues from a much wider perspective.

There is an old management formula that suggests:

Performance = f(ability X motivation X opportunity)

The essence of this 'formula' is that performance is not just about the ability to do the job but also the motivational interest and attitude of the individual together with the organisationally created opportunity or climate to perform. Too often, managers focus on the 'ability' factor (which is made up of education and relevant experience), without carefully examining the level of motivation of the person or considering whether the culture of the organisation allows this candidate the opportunity to perform.

Seasoned managers also add *attitude* to the list as an essential to the overall mix. Their experience tells them that no matter how much ability an employee might have, it is worth very little if they have a poor or disinterested attitude. Interviewing to explore a candidate's attitude is more difficult than confirming their education or experience.

The issue of whether candidates must have all the necessary *knowledge* to do the job is an interesting one. Certainly, if I was going to have heart transplant in the morning I would want to be sure that the surgeon had all the requisite knowledge! On the other hand, there may be some roles where innate ability and attitude are far more important than knowledge – where knowledge can be relatively easily imparted soon after joining the organisation. It is interesting to observe some major consulting firms and other large employers of college graduates preferring history or English 'majors' rather than students of business and finance. Their attitude seems to be: give us very bright, very broadly educated young men and women and we will teach them how to be consultants; we will coach them on how to use our tried and trusted methodologies.

I have talked to managers after they interviewed candidates that they turned down. When I explored why they disqualified these candidates, they replied that the candidate did not know X; that their course did not cover Y. I believe that for certain jobs, particularly at graduate level, you should be looking not at knowledge *per se* (that can be imparted soon after joining the organisation) but at the candidate's ability to think logically, be quick on the uptake ('a quick study') and have a good positive, enthusiastic attitude towards themselves and their careers ahead of them.

> *You should select for good attitude and train for skills.*
> *It's very tough to do it the other way around.*
> Frank, HR, High-Tech, US

Poor Questioning Technique

Even with good planning and broad focus, serious mistakes can be made through poor execution of the interview.

The interview is a conversation with a purpose. That purpose is to facilitate and encourage a flow of relevant information that will help you judge whether the candidate has the necessary abilities and motivation to be successful in the job. You need to control the conversation so that the candidate does most of the talking – up to 80% of the time. Your job is to make sure that the talking is highly relevant to your vacancy and presents you with plenty of opportunity to get further insight into the candidate's ability and motivation. You need to maintain control of the interview at all times by the use of appropriate technique.

Modern interview theory is based on a single universally held principle: past performance and behaviour in similar work and setting is the single most reliable predictor of future performance and behaviour in a given job. Thus it should not be surprising that there is a trend in employment interviewing towards behaviour-based questions.

Behaviour-based questions are not as difficult as they might first sound:

- Get the candidate to explain how he / she handled a particular challenge at work.
- Then follow up with questions that probe, such as "Why did you take that approach?" or "Did you consider other alternatives?" Follow-up with questions to get them to reflect back, "If you were faced with the same problem today, what if anything would you do differently?
- Outline a hypothetical scenario, which is relevant to the vacancy and designed to simulate a typical problem that the candidate might encounter in the job.
- Then ask the candidate how they might deal with the hypothetical situation. Follow up with questions like "Why take that approach?" or "When would you take action?"

The best friends of a good interviewer are Rudyard Kipling's 'six honest servingmen': What, Why, When, How, Where and Who.

An eminent Japanese professor once told me that you should ask *why* five times. His point was to continue to dig deeper, almost like removing layers of the onion: "Why did you do that?" Wait for the response then dig further "And why was that?" Response, followed by another "And why was that?" and so on.

Probing questions are essential to get further details and ensure that you get all the relevant facts. Examples of probing questions include:

- "What exactly was your role in the project?"
- "What were the challenges you met in that project?"
- "Could you describe in detail the process you use for …?"
- "What do you think are the strengths of that process?"
- "What do you think are the weaknesses in using that process?"
- "You said you had experience in …. Tell me more about that"
- "What do you like most in your current job?"
- "What do you like least in your current job?"

Ask for practical examples following a broad or generalised statement: "Interesting! Can you give me an example of that?"

Your pause or silence (a 'pregnant pause') can be a highly effective probe in compelling the candidate to talk further on the topic. Your silence usually compels the candidate to fill the void and add further comments, sometimes less 'processed' than before.

Introduce a probing question with some self-disclosure: "I sometimes get frustrated with my boss's style. What are some of the things that frustrate you about your boss?" Again, follow up with lots of "Why" questions.

Open questions are designed to get the candidate to talk: "Tell me about the time …?" or "What do you know about X?" or "What do you like most about your current job?" or "In what way do you think your experience matches the job that you have applied for?" All of these questions invite the candidate to open up and talk.

Closed questions are not very helpful unless you are looking for a definite "Yes" or "No" answer. A question such as "I see here that you have graduated from the London School of Economics" is really no more than a comment and is likely to generate a "Yes" response, which will add precious little to what you already know. Closed questions are best kept to clarify a point of fact: "Did you actually graduate from the course?"

A candidate's motivation can be difficult to assess but some thoughtful questions may draw out clues about the candidate's level of motivation – for example:

- "Why did you take that course?"
- "Were there subjects on the course that you disliked?"
- "How did you get through those subjects?"
- "What project did you do in your final year?"
- "Why did you pick that one?"
- "By the time you finished the project, what had you learnt about yourself?"
- "What difficulties did you first experience in your current job?"
- "How did you surmount those difficulties?
- "What aspects of your job performance are you least satisfied with and what are you doing about it?"
- "What motivates you most about your current job?"
- "What motivates you least about your current job and why?"
- "Thinking about bosses you have had in the past, what kind of boss motivates you?"
- "Why do you think that is?"

In conducting your interview, it is important to be able to balance being flexible enough to be able to explore emerging information during the interview with having a basic structure that you will follow. Being too *structured* will not permit you to follow a new line of enquiry; being too *flexible* will not permit you to cover all aspects you planned in the allocated time.

Making Your Selection

Now armed with your job description and a clear understanding of the vital few essential competencies necessary to be successful in the job, compare and contrast each of your candidates against that list of capabilities.

Analyse the candidate's CV / résumé and your interview notes and your impressions. Look for patterns and inconsistencies. Satisfy yourself that the candidate demonstrated sufficient motivation to want to do a good job. Compare each candidate against the specifications to be successful in the job. Compare them to the yardstick you have set. It is a common error in selection to pick the best candidate, even if that candidate does not measure up to your yardstick. If they do not measure up, then do not hire and go look again.

Your final decision may be subject to formal HR procedures around reference checking and medical examinations. These procedures are best left to those relevant professional departments.

Legal Matters

Legal compliance on selection practices and procedures in different countries is beyond the scope of this book. You need to be properly familiar with and clearly abide by the laws of the country in which you operate pertaining to such matters as race, gender, religion, sexual orientation, disability, age, etc., in interviewing and selecting candidates, together with legal compliance on data protection legislation.

Conclusion

A poor selection decision will result in you spending a disproportionate of your time managing your poor employee, addressing performance issues.

Take time out to carefully explore the position you are recruiting for and be clear on the essential skills and competencies necessary to be successful in the position.

Finally, the interview is a conversation with a purpose. That purpose is to facilitate and encourage a flow of relevant information that will help you judge whether the candidate has the necessary abilities and motivation to be successful in the job.

CHAPTER 10

MANAGING CHANGE

It would be understandable for you to believe that, as a new manager, you will not be called upon to manage major organisational change, at least in the short term. The reality however, is different. Your very promotion represents a significant change for your employees, one you certainly need to manage effectively!

Change

As you well know, one of the few certainties in life is change. Changes in organisational life driven by external factors including: changes in customer expectations; competitors; global macro-economics and government policy; developments in technology; and changes in social, cultural values and fashion.

Add to that list the internal drivers of change including: mergers and acquisitions; corporate reorganisations; appointment of new senior management; office / facility relocations; new product or service introductions and so on. The list is endless.

Respected business author and organisational anthropologist, Charles Handy[10] offers a provocative, if somewhat graphic, metaphor for organisational change: if you put a frog into a pot of cold water and heat it very slowly, the frog will let itself be boiled to death. Handy's metaphor warns that our business environment, just like the temperature of the pot with the frog, is constantly changing, sometimes imperceptibly so, and the

---

[10] Handy, C. (1995). *The Age of Unreason*, London: Arrow.

organisation needs to be aware of even subtle changes in their environment and be able to respond to those changes and opportunities accordingly or, as with the frog, it too will not survive.

The ability of an organisation and its managers to manage change effectively is a real source of capacity for survival and indeed for competitive advantage. The opposite also is true.

Accepting Change

Managers are no different from anybody else. Some recognise the need for ongoing change and improvement and embrace it, while others either through inertia or fear really struggle with it. A fundamental for managing change is accepting the change yourself. In your new role, much change will be initiated by more senior management and your role is to understand the need for the change and to support it. You need to be able to anticipate your employees' reaction to the proposed change and, if you believe they will be resistant, then find ways and means to reduce that resistance.

There is no room for a manager who openly expresses disagreement with a change initiative and is disparaging towards senior management, seeking to convince his or her employees of the errors of the proposed change. Equally, there is no room for the manager who, keeping his head down, is much more subtle and crafty in his efforts to thwart, or be passive-aggressive towards the initiative.

It is only natural that, while you will be open to and accept much change, there may be times when you will be uncomfortable with or disagree with a particular change. In the event that you are called on to manage a change that you disagree with, you should professionally explain your reservations and concerns to your own manager. If you are unsuccessful in convincing him / her otherwise, you now must try to get on with managing the change as professionally as you can (unless of course you feel there is a fundamental ethical issue at stake). There is no need for you to tell your employees of your reservations. However, if somehow your employees know that you are unhappy with the change and query you, then consider explaining to your employees that yes, you had some reservations, which you have discussed with senior management and that now you are going to support the change and get on with it, and that you expect your employees to do the same.

Barriers to Change

Barriers to organisational change are endless! They include basic inertia; an 'if it ain't broke' attitude; perceived threats to position; power and influence; fear that they will not have the necessary skills to perform new responsibilities; and / or deeply embedded countercultures – the list is endless. For many employees, including many managers, change is neither sought nor welcomed. People can find it disruptive and possibly intrusive and it can easily upset people's comfort zones.

People have different tolerance thresholds to change. Some people, by their very nature, are conservative or may have 'scartissue' from previous change efforts that have eroded their trust in management, whether in their current or previous employment; others are excited by the change perhaps because they see potential opportunity. There are also others who are not necessarily happy about the change but who recognise the threat and understand the implications of not changing and are therefore prepared to change.

Change Is a Transition not an Event

At a human level, managing change is first and foremost about the psychological process we go through to come to terms with a changed situation. It is something of a paradox but change starts not with beginnings but with endings. Change finally begins with the acceptance that things are changing and acceptance of the need to leave the old situation behind.

Once you understand that transition begins with letting go of something, you have taken the first step in managing change for yourself. The second step is to help your employees to let go.

> *Habit is habit and not to be flung out the window by any man, but coaxed downstairs one step at a time.*
> Mark Twain

Managing Change

Managing change requires some essential skills and actions. Some of these have already been dealt with in earlier chapters but are summarised here.

Clear Leadership

Have a clear understanding of what you want to change and the compelling reason for it.

When leading change in your group, you will need to show clear leadership to get people to 'sign-up' for the change. In the first instance, this will require you to lead by example; your employees will watch you carefully to see what signals you are sending. If your employees do not see you actively engaging with the change or clearly 'walking the talk' yourself, do not be surprised if you do not engender much enthusiasm and commitment for the change on the part of others. Any sign of lack of your commitment on your part is likely to raise doubts and possibly erode confidence and undermine the whole change effort.

In leading change in your group, it is important to establish some sense of urgency. Be sure to highlight the potential opportunities or threats and explain clearly the consequences of not changing.

Build Support for the Change

Convince and persuade formal and informal opinion leaders of the importance of the change. 'Managing by influence' is an important activity to lay the ground-work and build support for the change (**Chapter 6**). There are clear interdependencies between departments and groups in most organisations and your success will very much depend on your capacity to influence and persuade people outside of your direct chain of command. Creating supportive alliances and networks both inside and outside your organisation are essential to the success of your change initiative. Understand who the key opinion leaders are, who the likely supporters and objectors are and build your compelling case for change with them.

In the event that you can identify people with formal or informal influence who are unlikely to support the change, consider inviting them to be part of a benchmarking process to go out and experience, first-hand, some of the compelling need for change – for example, customer visits, visits to an industry leader, etc. Sometimes your most resistant employees become the strongest champions for change once you have helped them to see the light.

However, even with that effort, you may find an employee or two who are still resistant to the change. As long as these employees are not central to the change itself consider working around them. It may be that they are just slower in accepting change. However, if they are central to the change and after all your efforts are still resistant to it, then you may be left with no

option but to deal with the matter as a performance issue
(**Chapter 7**).

> *One time a new senior manager was driving a major*
> *change and while most of the managers were supportive*
> *of the change, a couple were not. After some effort on his*
> *part over a month or so, he finally gave up the*
> *persuasion route and declared to the full team, "Ladies*
> *and Gentlemen, the train is leaving the station now.*
> *You are either on the train or standing on the platform.*
> *There will be no more discussion. You must decide and*
> *decide now"… They got on board pretty quickly after*
> *that!*
> Jean, Supply Chain, Pharma, UK

Involvement & Participation

Involve people as early as possible in the change process.
Whenever you can, let people participate in decision-making.
While you know *what* has to change, it usually makes sense to
involve relevant employees in determining the *how* the change
should be implemented. Having said that, in involving your
employees, you need to be very clear about the parameters
around options, the selection criteria for decision-making and
the necessary timeframes for decisions to be made.

It often has been suggested that fear of the unknown is a barrier
to change and indeed, in some situations, it can be. But consider
Peter de Jager's advice:

> *If people were afraid of the unknown they might not want to learn*
> *how to drive. Yet most people can't wait to learn and get behind*
> *the wheel of a car. People don't necessarily reject change. What*
> *they resent is being changed.*[11]

---

[11] Peter de Jager on change management, www.technobility.com.

Where you can, ask for ideas and seek suggestions. Sometimes your most resistant employees become champions of the change once they are involved and become engaged in the process.

Effective Communication

John Kotter suggests that the three most important actions in managing change are communications, communications and communications.

Some managers feel that the communications job is done once they pin a notice on the notice board. As previously noted, effective communications is about *reception*, not *transmission*. Effective managers turn boring and often unread notices into regular open dialogue about the planned change. These managers engage in conversation with their employees and stitch the message into day-to-day discussions, making sure employees really understand the nature of the change, why it is important, and how it will affect them.

> " *I think some managers only communicate what is going to change. They hardly spend any time explaining why the change is necessary. My experience has always been that if employees understand the rationale for the change … the 'why' if you like, they are much more likely to be supportive of the change.* "
> Jean, Supply Chain Manager, Pharma, UK

Training

One of the reasons employees sometimes resist change is because they do not feel they have the required skills for their new responsibilities and feel insecure in their positions in the face of the change. Organisational change often requires some employee training and education. Educational activities can help employees understand the need for the change and can build greater commitment to it. They also provide a sense of psychological safety to employees as they show the organisation's intention to support them through the change by building confidence in their own ability to deal with it.

As you plan your change initiative, carefully consider and assess the necessary training and education your employees will require and put a plan in place to complete that programme at the relevant point. Other support departments may be responsible for the provision of the programme but your responsibility is to ensure that it is provided effectively to your team.

Detailed Implementation Plan

They say that the road to hell is paved with good intentions. Being clear on *what* needs to change is one thing; being clear on *how* the change will be managed is something else altogether. Not to have a clear plan is tantamount to 'management by wishful thinking'. The plan must spell out the key steps, the sequence of those steps, clear accountability for the steps and a time-table.

Once the plan is up and running, make sure that it continues to schedule. You need an effective process to monitor progress; you also need some contingency plans. Having said all of that, while carefully monitoring progress, always be mindful of achieving some balance between managing and meddling, trusting your team to make good progress *but* keeping an eye on that progress.

Conclusion

Change is indeed one of life's certainties. You can embrace or fight it. But fighting it is like standing on a beach with a small bucket and trying to bail back an incoming tide. As you grow your managerial career, your skills in leading and managing change will undoubtedly become a career-defining competency.

CHAPTER 11

CONTINUING TO LEARN

Even before I started writing I knew that, by the time I finished writing this book, I would want to go back and edit and change much of the earlier chapters. As we learn and reflect, we constantly refine and develop our insights and skills based on what we learn. The road to mastering your managerial capability is essentially a learning process that will take place over time. It is a bit of a cliché but it is true that learning is a journey and it follows that developing to be a good manager too is a journey, never a destination.

How Do Managers Learn?

Every day there is opportunity for learning. Some learning is from explicit input such as coaching or seminars. However, most learning as adults is from experience.

Learn from Mistakes ... Preferably Other People's Mistakes

Moving into a management position is a learning transition. In that learning situation, it is inevitable that mistakes will be made. However, if you have to learn from mistakes, it is better that you learn from other people's mistakes. It is safer and a whole lot less painful.

> *I often have heard it said that the school of hard knocks provides an excellent education but learning from others is cheaper tuition. It's so true!*
> Frank, HR Director, High-Tech, US

Learn from Feedback

Your development as a manager will not happen in a vacuum. Learning from feedback and coaching from your boss and supportive peers can be highly effective. Do not wait for the annual appraisal process; ask your boss and a few colleagues who are well positioned to observe your behaviour and skills. Candid and supportive feedback is highly effective. Query and test your assumptions with them to check that you are on the right path.

Keep Up-to-Date

While most learning happens on the job, it is essential that you keep your technical expertise and industry knowledge up-to-date. You are unlikely to hold the respect of your team or of your customer if they feel that you are not up-to-speed with relevant trends and developments.

Social networking is exploding and can be highly effective in keeping up-to-date with technical and industry developments.

The work demands of a busy manager leaves little time for lots of reading of management journals or attending seminars. Ask for recommendations for one good journal or occasional book. Make a deal with a couple of colleagues that you will circulate and swop, by exception, useful articles from the journals. In the case of books, scan the table of contents and identify the few interesting chapters.

An advantage of an occasional seminar, besides the content, is the opportunity to quietly reflect on important issues away from the daily 'coal-face' of operational demands. Consider industry association or professional bodies (management institutes), many of which run short, local, often free breakfast or early evening seminars.

Learn from Regular Reflection

At the end of a project, ask yourself the question "If I had to do that again, what would I do differently and why?" Reflect on something you admired in the way your boss or a peer managed a particular project or handled a particularly difficult meeting; ask yourself what you could learn from it. Equally, where a project or meeting was not managed well, consider what went wrong and how you might have approached things differently. Observe a particular behaviour by your boss or a peer and watch the effect the behaviour has on other people, good or bad.

Learning from experience is gradual absorption; it is learning by osmosis. Whether it is from experience, observing others, feedback or seminars, learning needs to be part of your ongoing agenda; a daily routine. Taking the briefest time each day to reflect on what you are learning and what you need to learn will pay rich dividends for you over time.

> *The world is changing; technology is changing. I need opportunities to learn and not fall behind. I want to create a similar environment where my employees feel they are learning all the time and that they are open to change.*
> Jean, Supply Chain Manager, Pharma, UK

Complement Your Strengths and Weaknesses

Even with the best management education and powers of reflection, you will have both strengths and weaknesses. Make sure that you have people in your team who complement your strengths, weaknesses and preferred style of operating. Identify individuals to work with you who can and will cover any gaps.

If you are more strategic and big picture in your thinking, then make sure you have others in the team who understand all the details. But having them on your team is pointless unless you listen to them.

In contrast, if you like to engage in lots and lots of detail, make sure you have somebody in your team who can get you to look up on occasion to see and understand the 'big picture'. If you are more operational and logic driven, make sure others in the team can balance that with concerns about people issues and that can champion their cause.

Transition into Management is Challenging *and* Exciting

Much of what you do as a manager you do with other people. Keep in mind the potential impact you have on their career and even their lives. Do your job. After all, that is what you are paid for. But do it with a balanced focus on the goals to be achieved *together* with a sense of humanity. You can strive for the goal and, at the same time, preserve people's dignity at work. You are likely to have to make some tough decisions along the way. Facing up to those decisions is one thing; how you go about executing them is something different. Having some empathy and understanding for people does not make you a weak manager. Equally, being tough does not make you a strong manager, or rather an effective manager, over the long haul. Often, people do not leave jobs, they leave poor managers. It is all about balance.

> *Sometime after I was promoted as a manager, I came to realise that there were two very different dimensions to my new job. There was the definite and tangible dimension where I was now responsible for production, quality levels, and R&D activities that had to be completed and so on. I clearly had all of these responsibilities on my shoulders. There was however, another, more intangible dimension: this was the realisation that ultimately I was responsible. Previously, there was always someone to go to; somebody else who would carry the ultimate responsibility for the decision. This more intangible dimension includes being responsible for the way your group works together and you are also now centrally involved in their individual career hopes and dreams.*
> Timothy, Manufacturing Operations, Ireland

There is no doubt that the transition into management is challenging but it is also exciting. It *is* about swinging on the trapeze; letting go of that bar, flying through the air, and then grabbing the new challenge. This transition is very much your launch pad to develop your managerial career.

> *To become a pilot, you have to learn to fly. Otherwise, you can't be a pilot. Similarly, to become a manager, you have to learn to manage. Otherwise, you won't be a successful manager.*
> Kevin, Senior Manager, Government Agency, Ireland

In promoting you, your organisation has given you a huge vote of confidence. They obviously believe in you. Do not be afraid! What you need to understand is that your job has changed in a most fundamental way and be aware of the skills you need to develop and to make sure you have people on your team who can complement your strengths and weaknesses.

> *It's a great privilege to lead others. Some see it as a*
> *bundle of trouble but for me, it's a fantastic opportunity*
> *to make a difference. Having the opportunity to lead*
> *people and look to get the best out of them is probably*
> *one of the highest honours in life.*
> Gene, Regional Director, Pharma, South-East Asia

Congratulations on your promotion. If you make a real success of this first transition into management, I am confident that it will not be your last promotion.

ABOUT THE AUTHOR

Patrick Cunneen has well over three decades' experience as a manager, teacher and management coach, across three continents.

Until his retirement in 2002, Pat was Director of Human Resources for Worldwide Manufacturing at Analog Devices Inc. (ADI), with strategic HR responsibilities for manufacturing locations in Massachusetts, California, Ireland, Taiwan, Japan and the Philippines. Previously, from 1987 to 1990, Pat was Director of HR for ADI in Wilmington, MA and, from 1976 to 1987, was HR Director during the start-up of ADI's Irish Division. Other experience includes De Beers, Shannon Development Company, Wyeth Nutritionals and Abu Dhabi Aircraft Technologies.

He is a founder and director of Lighthouse Organisational Consultants Ltd., a consultancy firm specialising in organisational development, HR consulting, organisational change and executive coaching. He has been Adjunct Professor of Human Resource Management at the University of Limerick and a regular contributor on strategy and human resources programmes at the Irish Management Institute and at the Irish Police College. He also has been involved in start-up and small business support.

Pat has a BComm degree from University College Dublin, an MBS from the University of Limerick and is a Fellow of the Chartered Institute of Personnel & Development. His first book, *Organisational Structure: An Essential Lever in Managing Change*, was published in 2008.

ABOUT OAK TREE PRESS

Oak Tree Press develops and delivers information, advice and resources for entrepreneurs and managers. It is Ireland's leading business book publisher, with an unrivalled reputation for quality titles across business, management, HR, law, marketing and enterprise topics. NuBooks is its recently-launched imprint, publishing short, focused ebooks for busy entrepreneurs and managers.

In addition, through its founder and managing director, Brian O'Kane, Oak Tree Press occupies a unique position in start-up and small business support in Ireland through its standard-setting titles, as well training courses, mentoring and advisory services.

Oak Tree Press is comfortable across a range of communication media – print, web and training, focusing always on the effective communication of business information.

Oak Tree Press, 19 Rutland Street, Cork, Ireland.
T: + 353 21 4313855 F: + 353 21 4313496.
E: info@oaktreepress.com W: www.oaktreepress.com.